April 7th, 1805. Our vessels consisted of six small canoes, and two large perogues. This little fleet, altho' not quite so rispectable as those of Columbus or Capt. Cook were still viewed by us with as much pleasure as those deservedly famed adventurers ever beheld theirs.

MERIWETHER LEWIS

LEWIS & CLARK
ADVENTURES WEST

BY JOHN C. HAMILTON

Published by Sparrow Media Group, Inc., P.O. Box 44272, Eden Prairie, Minnesota 55344-4272.
Copyright ©2004 by Sparrow Media Group, Inc. International copyrights reserved in all countries.
No part of this book may be reproduced in any form without written permission from the publisher.

Printed and bound in the United States of America.
First edition, 2004.

Edited by Paul Abdo
Graphic Design: John C. Hamilton

www.sparrowmediagroup.com

Library of Congress Cataloging-in-Publication Data

Hamilton, John C., 1959-
    Lewis and Clark: Adventures West / John C. Hamilton
    1st ed. -- Eden Prairie, Minn: Sparrow Media Group, Inc., 2004.
    192 p. : ill.
    Includes bibliographical references and index.
    Summary: Joins the Lewis and Clark Expedition in the spring of 1804 as they set out to explore
the Louisiana Purchase. Includes highlights and directions to historical points of interest.
    ISBN 0-9719304-2-2
    1. Lewis and Clark Expedition (1804-1806)—Juvenile literature. 2. West (U.S.)—Discovery
and exploration—Juvenile literature. 3. West (U.S.)—Description and travel—Juvenile literature.
4. Lewis, Meriwether, 1774-1809—Juvenile literature. 5. Clark, William, 1770-1838—Juvenile
literature. [1. Lewis and Clark Expedition (1804-1806) 2. West (U.S.)—Discovery and
exploration. 3. Lewis, Meriwether, 1774-1809 4. Clark, William, 1770-1838.] I. Title.

    F592.7.H257 2003
    917.804'2—dc21

2003090920

Dust jacket design and photography:
John C. Hamilton

For Sue

FOREWORD

Over the years, I've become quite well acquainted with Lewis and Clark and the men (and one woman) of the Corps of Discovery. I've traveled their trail many times, from Monticello to the Pacific Ocean. Like most people today, I've used modern means of transportation on today's highways, but I've also covered many miles of scenic trail from a canoe or from the saddle of a horse.

Always I marvel at what the Lewis and Clark expedition accomplished. I try to envision what they would have seen, before the days of power lines, highways, fences and cities. We can only guess what thoughts went through their minds. At times the journals give us clues. Descriptive entries in the journals of campsites and landmarks give us a glimpse of what they were thinking: Camp Fortunate; Camp Disappointment; Bad Humored Island; Colt Killed Creek; Hungry Creek; Camp Pleasant. Who can forget Clark's exclamation when he first sighted the Pacific: "Ocian in view! O! the joy!" If only we could have been with them (could I have kept up?).

Few people today are aware that during the years of 1803-1806, three other expeditions were sent by the Jefferson Administration to explore land west of the Mississippi River. Two of these expeditions are virtually unknown today. In 1804, the Dunbar-Hunter expedition explored Arkansas' Washita River. In 1806, the Freeman-Custis Expedition explored the Red River into Texas. The third expedition was Zebulon Pike's, which we've all heard of, but know little about.

Only the Lewis and Clark Expedition has an organized following. The Lewis and Clark Trail Heritage Foundation, now 34 years old, has national offices and staff in Great Falls, MT. It has 40 or more chapters spread from coast to coast, a growing membership, and publishes a quarterly magazine, as well as a quarterly newsletter. It holds annual meetings somewhere along the trail every summer.

The Lewis and Clark Expedition of 1803-1806 has caught the interest of the American people. Hundreds of books have been written about the Corps of Discovery, as well as movies, videos and made-for-TV documentaries. Our new dollar coin bears the likeness of Sacagawea and her baby. Our new nickel will, for the years 2003-2006, have a Lewis and Clark design on the obverse.

There is something about Lewis and Clark that makes us want to know more about them, what they accomplished, and the Native Americans they met on their epic 8,000-mile journey. They were more than explorers. They were scientists, botanists, zoologists, ethnologists, geographers, doctors, and, most of all, ambassadors to the 50 Indian nations they encountered. Lewis and Clark never would have succeeded had it not been for the help given them by the Native Americans they met along the way.

They were the first Europeans to see much of the land they explored, but equally important they were also among the last to see it in its unaltered state before it was changed forever. Following them, hard on their heels, were trappers, traders, farmers, ranchers, miners, loggers, soldiers, hunters, and eventually, society as we know it today.

Read about Lewis and Clark. Explore their trail and enjoy the journey. You too may become a follower of the Corps of Discovery.

Ron Laycock
Benson, MN
April, 2003

Ron Laycock is the president (August 2003-2004) of the Lewis and Clark Trail Heritage Foundation (www.lewisandclark.org). An avid Lewis & Clark historian, he leads canoe trips and bus tours along the trail, and is a frequent guest speaker at schools. In 2001 he received the Distinguished Service Award from the foundation.

CONTENTS

e rocks. the shell is thin and consists of one valve
a small circular apperture is formed in the center of
the under shell. the animal is soft & boneless. –

The white salmon Trout which we had previously
seen only at the great falls of the Columbia has
now made it's appearance in the creeks near
this place. one of them was brought us today by an Indian who had just
taken it with his gig. this is a

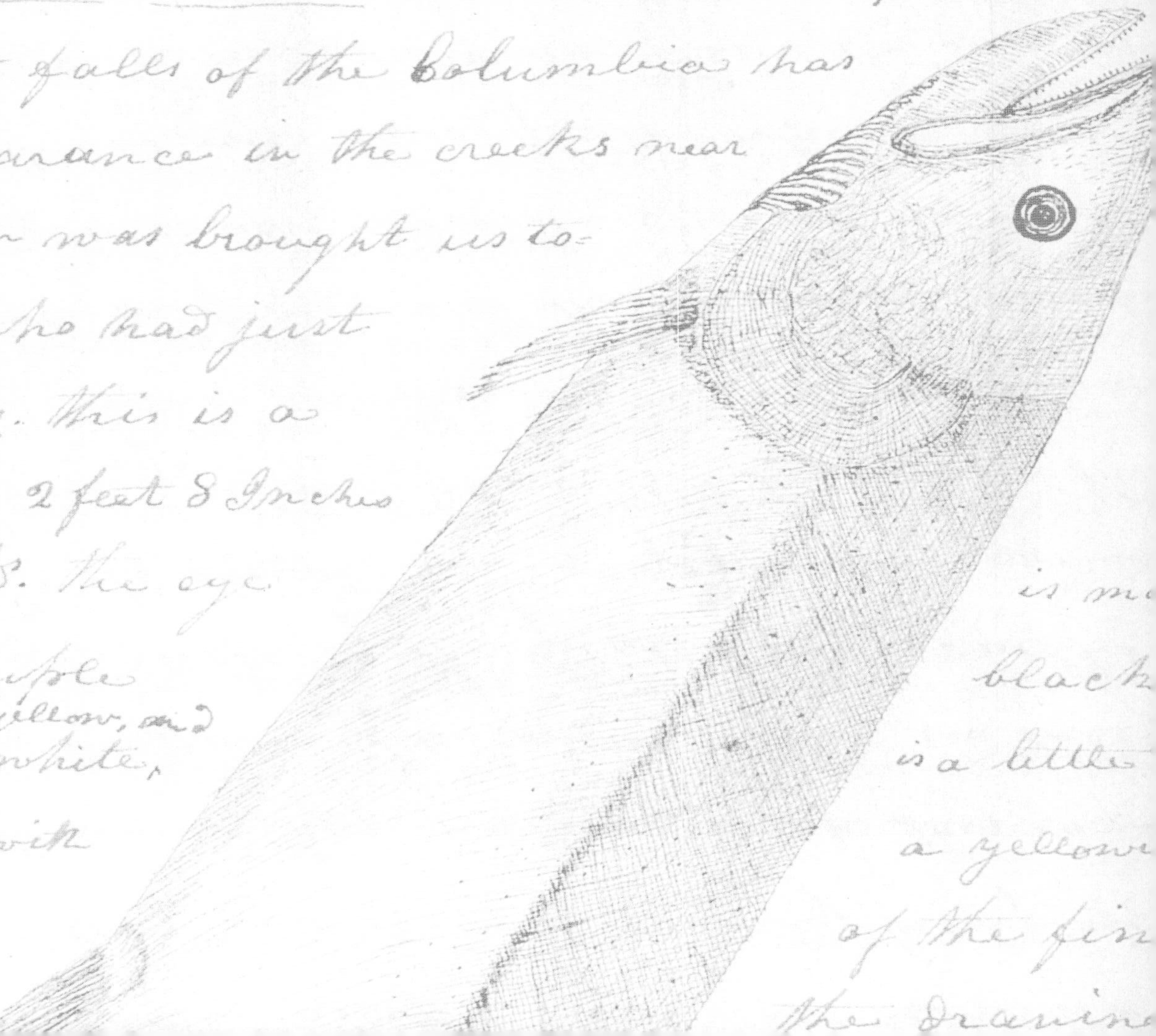

likeness of it; it was 2 feet 8 Inches
long, and weighed 10 lbs. the eye is mo
derately large, the puple black
with a small admixture of yellow, and
nd iris of a silvery white, is a little
rbid near it's border with a yellow
rown. the position of the fin
ay be seen from the drawin

PART ONE
THE CORPS OF DISCOVERY

Honored Parence,

    I am now on an expidition to the westward, with Capt. Lewis and Capt. Clark . . . through the interior parts of North America. We are to ascend the Missouri River with a boat as far as it is navigable and then go by land, to the western ocean, if nothing prevents. . . .

    We expect to be gone 18 months or two years. We are to receive a great reward for this expidition, when we return.

    I . . . will write next winter if I have a chance.

SERGEANT JOHN ORDWAY

EXPLORERS

O n a spring afternoon in 1804, three boats loaded with about 45 men and supplies pushed off from the east shore of the Mississippi River just upstream from the frontier town of St. Louis. The tiny flotilla, consisting of a keelboat and two boats resembling very large canoes, crossed the Mississippi and entered the mouth of the Missouri River. The men strained their oars against the powerful and muddy current.

The explorers called themselves the Corps of Discovery. They were young men entering uncharted lands at the request of President Thomas Jefferson. Led by two extraordinary commanders, they would travel thousands of miles through plains filled with vast herds of wild animals, across rugged mountains, and down rivers teeming with fish.

Prairie grass on the Great Plains, North Dakota.

Bison grazing on the Great Plains of North Dakota.

They would meet dozens of Native American tribes, many of whom had never before seen white men. The expedition was armed with the most advanced weapons available. But even though they would tell the Indians their land was no longer their own, they would be met more often by kindness than anger, generosity more than mistrust. Several times, when danger and misfortune threatened to break apart the expedition, these soldier-explorers would be rescued by the compassion of others.

They would be the first American citizens to gaze upon the vastness of the Great Plains; first to cross the Continental Divide; first to struggle over snow-capped peaks until they reached rivers that ran westward. Pushing on, they would be the first Americans to reach the Pacific Ocean overland from the east.

Two U.S. Army officers, very different from each other, led the Corps of Discovery. Captain Meriwether Lewis was the commander, the planner, the scientist. Captain William Clark was the steady one, the mapmaker, the leader of men. They were both superb woodsmen. They were great friends, and their skills complemented each other perfectly. Within a few months they molded their men into an efficient unit that followed orders and carried out tasks with precision. The men of the Corps worked as a team, and they would follow Lewis and Clark anywhere.

After more than 8,000 miles (12,875 km) and nearly two and a half years of exploration, the Corps of Discovery would fail in its mission to find the fabled Northwest Passage, the easy, long-sought trade route to the Pacific Ocean. But Lewis and Clark succeeded in bringing back a wealth of discoveries—122 new kinds of animals, 178 new plants. They made contact with dozens of Native American tribes. They strengthened the United States's claim on the North American continent. And just as importantly, the Corps of Discovery fired the imagination of a nation. They blazed the trail that would soon be followed by legions of trappers, traders, and settlers.

The Lewis and Clark expedition is a story of dedication and courage, friendship and teamwork. In many ways, it's the story of America.

Artist Olaf Seltzer painted this scene of Meriwether Lewis climbing a ridge on May 26, 1805. "From this point," Lewis wrote, "I beheld the Rocky Mountains for the first time."

However our present interests may restrain us within our own limits, it is impossible not to look forward to distant times, when our rapid multiplication will expand itself beyond those limits and cover the whole . . . continent, with a people speaking the same language, governed in similar forms and by similar laws.

THOMAS JEFFERSON
FIRST INAUGURAL ADDRESS

LOOK FORWARD TO DISTANT TIMES

On March 4, 1801, Thomas Jefferson took office as the third president of the United States. The young country contained just over five million people—20 percent of those were African-American slaves. Two thirds of American citizens lived within 50 miles (80 km) of the Atlantic Ocean. Settlers were pushing westward beyond the Appalachian Mountains, but there were only a handful of roads reaching into the new territories. There were no telephones or telegraphs. Letters and packages traveled at the speed of a horse, sometimes taking several weeks to reach far-off destinations. United States territory ended at the eastern banks of the Mississippi River.

Beyond the Mississippi, reaching all the way to the Rocky Mountains, lay a vast and largely unknown area called Louisiana.

(Today's state of Louisiana is just a small part of the former territory.) Nobody really knew what was in Louisiana. Scattered Indian tribes lived there; only a few fur trappers had ever ventured into its outer edges.

Thomas Jefferson knew that his young country's destiny depended on exploring the unknown lands west of the Mississippi River.

To the south and west, New Spain stretched from Florida to Texas, all the way to the California coast. England controlled territory to the north, in Canada. English traders and trappers were already starting outposts, pushing into Minnesota and the Dakotas. English ships cruised up and down the coastlines of the Pacific Northwest, and Russians were building forts in Alaska. All of these countries wanted to control the western reaches of the North American continent. Whoever won the race would lay claim to all the riches and vast opportunity of that unknown land.

After the American Revolution, there were at least four attempts to find the headwaters of the Missouri River. Once found, the explorers would seek a short portage over low mountains until reaching the Columbia River, which flows west to the Pacific Ocean. (Most people assumed the hike would be like crossing the Appalachian Mountains. Actually, the Rocky Mountains are much more rugged. Some western peaks soar twice as high as Virginia's Blue Ridge Mountains, which were thought at the time to be the highest on the continent.)

Thomas Jefferson, one of America's Founding Fathers, organized three of these expeditions to explore the continent's interior. All were doomed to failure. A young man by the name of Meriwether Lewis, a neighbor of Jefferson's from Albemarle County in Virginia, once volunteered, but he was turned down because he was only 18 years old at the time.

President Jefferson was a brilliant politician. He was also a scientist with a great thirst for knowledge. At his Virginia home, Monticello, he collected a vast library. He was especially interested in natural history, taking delight in the discovery of new plants and animals.

In Jefferson's library were many books on the unexplored regions of North America. He owned more books on the subject than any library in the world. The books told of woolly mammoths, erupting volcanoes, and hills of pure salt. They also spoke of the fabled Northwest Passage, a mostly water route that cut through the continent, making it easy to send trade goods from coast to coast.

Jefferson had a grand dream that the United States would someday occupy the entire continent. He wanted to create a single nation, governed by democracy, which stretched from the Atlantic Ocean to the Pacific. Jefferson knew that commerce and trade would be the driving force to achieve his dream.

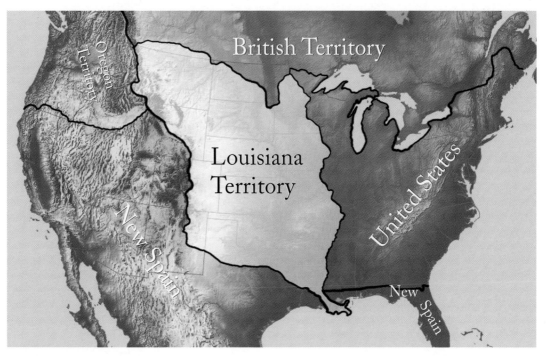

Like many people at the time, Jefferson believed the Northwest Passage existed. It would open up the country to fur traders and others who were eager to make money in the rich markets of the Orient. Without an easy overland route, eastern traders had to send ships on a long and dangerous journey, either around southern Africa or the tip of South America.

Jefferson knew that whichever country occupied the unexplored lands west of the Mississippi had a better chance of laying claim to them. This is why there was such a great push to explore, to get fur trapping established, and to make trading alliances with Native American tribes.

In 1793, Scotsman Alexander Mackenzie explored the southern reaches of Canada. He managed to cross the Continental Divide and make it to the Pacific Ocean. Mackenzie's explorations gave the British a toehold on the western regions, but his route wasn't very useful for trade because of the rugged mountain areas that had to be crossed.

Alarmed that the British had a head start exploring the inner continent, Jefferson proposed yet another expedition. It would be headed by his personal secretary, Meriwether Lewis, the same young man who years earlier had volunteered for one of Jefferson's other ill-fated expeditions. This time, he would blaze a trail through the heart of a continent.

Capt. Lewis is brave, prudent, habituated to the woods, & familiar with Indian manners & character. He is not regularly educated, but he possesses a great mass of accurate observation on all the subjects of nature which present themselves.

THOMAS JEFFERSON
LETTER TO DR. BENJAMIN RUSH, FEBRUARY 28, 1803

MERIWETHER LEWIS

*I*n early 1801, the presidential election was so close that Congress had to decide who won. Just before inauguration day, a divided Congress chose Thomas Jefferson over his bitter rival Aaron Burr. Once in office, Jefferson, a Republican, found himself surrounded by his political enemies, the Federalists. He needed someone he could trust as his personal secretary.

Meriwether Lewis was a young man in his late 20s. He grew up in Albemarle County in Virginia, not far from Jefferson's home at Monticello. Like Jefferson, Lewis was the son of a plantation owner. As with most Virginia plantations at the time, the main crop was tobacco, and the fields were worked by slaves.

When Lewis was a young boy of five, his father died serving in the Colonial Army during the Revolutionary War. His mother soon remarried and moved the family to her new husband's estate in Georgia.

Lewis loved the outdoors. He learned to fish and hunt by the time he was eight. He was moody and serious, self-reliant and sturdy. Although he was a fearless horse rider, he also loved to "ramble," walking endlessly through the woods. His mother taught him about wild plants that could be used as medicine. Through her, Lewis gained a love of learning.

Meriwether Lewis, in a painting by Charles Willson Peale. Lewis's outdoor skills, and his sharp powers of observation, convinced Thomas Jefferson that the young Virginian was the right man to lead the Corps of Discovery.

Lewis knew that he needed an education, that someday he would be responsible for the family's plantation. There weren't many schools back then. Many children of rich plantation owners went to live with teachers for a time. So, when he turned 13, Lewis moved back to Virginia and lived with a tutor. He loved to read. He studied botany, history, math, and geography. Although he still liked to roam alone in the woods, he worked hard at his studies.

After five years of schooling, Lewis was forced to stop his education. His mother's husband had died, and she needed assistance moving herself and Lewis's siblings back to the family plantation in Virginia. After helping her move, Lewis found himself in charge of the estate.

Taking care of a 2,000-acre (809-ha) plantation was a huge responsibility, and Lewis threw himself into it. He worked hard to make sure land was cleared, crops were planted and harvested, and all the day-to-day routines were taken care of.

Meriwether Lewis poses for artist Charles de Saint-Mémin after returning from the wilderness in 1806. The fur cape that he wore, which Lewis called *"the most eligant peice of Indian dress I ever saw,"* was a gift from Shoshone chief Cameahwait. The cape was made of otter skin trimmed with white weasel. The Corps visited the Shoshone tribe while camped near the Continental Divide in what is today southwestern Montana.

Lewis & Clark: Adventures West

Though he worked hard, the life of a Virginia plantation owner didn't suit Lewis very well. He wanted to roam in the woods again, to get out where he could spread his wings and explore. When he was 20, he joined the military. Lewis served as a United States Army officer on the wild frontiers of Pennsylvania and Ohio, honing his skill as a sharpshooter while traveling up and down the Ohio River.

In 1801 Thomas Jefferson called Lewis to Washington, D.C. The president hired the 28-year-old Virginian to be his personal secretary. Jefferson chose Lewis because he was a friend, a neighbor, and a good Republican, a rarity in the army. Jefferson wanted to get rid of Federalist officers that former President John Adams had appointed before leaving office. Jefferson had no army experience himself. Lewis, on the other hand, knew which officers would be loyal to the president.

As the president's sole aide, Lewis met some of the most powerful and influential people in the country. He also learned much of Jefferson's interest in the West, and the potential held in that immense, unexplored territory.

President Thomas Jefferson's home at Monticello, in Albemarle County, Virginia. Meriwether Lewis grew up near Monticello. He also spent time there while serving as the president's aide, planning for the Corps of Discovery.

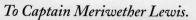

To Captain Meriwether Lewis.
The object of your mission is to explore the Missouri river,
& such principal stream of it, as, by it's course and communication
with the waters of the Pacific ocean . . . may offer the most direct
& practicable water communication across this continent for the
purposes of commerce.

THOMAS JEFFERSON
JUNE 20, 1803

THE OBJECT OF YOUR MISSION

*A*s Thomas Jefferson's personal secretary, Meriwether Lewis lived in the newly constructed White House for two years. During this time, the building was called the President's House. Later, the British burned the residence during the War of 1812. After the war it was repainted a bright white, which is why it is known today as the White House.

Jefferson was recently widowed, and his two daughters were grown and married. Lewis stayed in the East Room of the mansion. He ran errands for the president, copied official papers, and made lists of army officers he expected to remain loyal to Jefferson. Aside from the servants, Lewis and Jefferson were the only people to occupy the President's House. Lewis dined with the president nearly every night. Jefferson once wrote, "Capt. Lewis and myself are like two mice in a church."

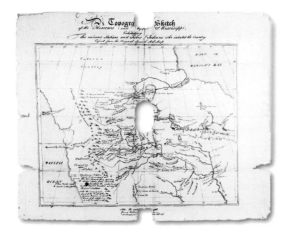

A Topographic Sketch of the Missouri and Upper Mississippi, by Antoine Soulard, in 1802, correctly showed the Missouri River heading toward the Rocky Mountains. Soulard was wrong, however, in representing the mountains as a single line of small bumps on the map. Thinking the Rockies to be a minor obstacle, Thomas Jefferson was determined to send the Corps of Discovery farther west than any expedition had ever before ventured, into the blank western areas of the map, the great unknown.

One hundred years after the Lewis and Clark expedition, photographer Edward S. Curtis made it his life's work to roam the West, documenting Native American culture. He took this image of Ogalala Sioux chief Red Hawk in the South Dakota Badlands in 1905.

Lewis learned the thorny details of diplomacy and politics during his stay with Jefferson. He rubbed elbows with Washington's elite, from powerful congressmen to foreign diplomats. As they grew closer, Jefferson became a father figure to Lewis. The president noted that Lewis was prone to dark moods that Jefferson called "depressions of the mind." But his confidence in the young Virginian never wavered.

On January 18, 1803, Jefferson sent a confidential letter to Congress. "The river Missouri," he wrote, "and the Indians inhabiting it, are not as well known as is rendered desirable. . . . An intelligent officer with ten or twelve chosen men . . . might explore the whole line, even to the Western Ocean."

Jefferson made the expedition more attractive to his Federalist rivals by emphasizing commercial gain. He also kept the cost low, only $2,500 to fund the entire expedition, although the cost would eventually climb to $38,722. On February 28, 1803, Congress approved the president's proposal. Jefferson was delighted. He chose his young aide, Meriwether Lewis, to lead the expedition. Lewis eagerly accepted.

Some people thought it was odd that Jefferson picked someone like Lewis to lead so important an expedition, but the president was confident in his choice. Jefferson wrote that Lewis was "brave, prudent, habituated to the woods, & familiar with Indian manners & character."

Over the next several months, Jefferson and Lewis made plans. Lewis would take several dozen men on a military mission Jefferson dubbed the *Corps of Discovery* (pronounced *core*). Besides searching for the Northwest Passage, they had several other goals. They would collect and describe any new plants and animals they discovered. They would map rivers and mountains, along with precise latitude and longitude measurements. They were to note the land's economic potential—how well it could be farmed, and if it contained precious minerals, like gold or silver. They were also to contact Indian nations, record their culture and customs, and bring them into a trade partnership with the United States.

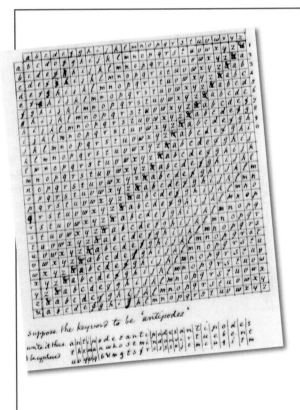

Thomas Jefferson worried that messages sent back from the Corps might be intercepted, especially by the English or Spanish, so he created this code matrix for Lewis to use. To decode a message, the sender and receiver decided in advance on a secret keyword, in this example, "artichokes." By knowing the keyword, the receiver could then look up the corresponding letters on the grid and descramble the coded message.

To test the code matrix with Lewis, an optimistic Jefferson wrote, *"I am at the head of the Missouri, all well, and the Indians so far friendly."* Despite taking this precaution, no records have been found of Lewis sending a coded message back to Thomas Jefferson.

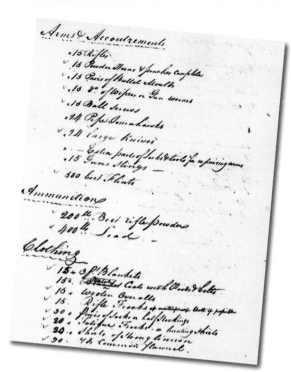

Lewis made many lists of supplies the expedition would need to complete its journey. This list details the guns, ammunition, and some of the clothing Lewis bought for the men of the Corps.

Jefferson sent Lewis to Philadelphia to train with some of the country's best scientists. Lewis learned how to preserve plant specimens, how to measure latitude and longitude, and how to identify fossils. He also learned medicine from one of the most famous doctors of the time, Dr. Benjamin Rush, who taught Lewis the importance of "bloodletting." By opening a sick person's vein and releasing blood, it was thought that toxins would be flushed away. Of course, today we know that this only makes matters worse, but at the time everyone believed that bloodletting helped most illnesses.

While in Philadelphia, Lewis kept busy collecting supplies for the expedition. The men would be completely out of touch with civilization for at least two years. Lewis purchased some preserved soup, but the men would have to hunt for most of their food. Lewis bought the most modern rifles available at the time, the Model 1803, the army's first standard-issue rifle. Lewis also bought an air rifle with his own money. The weapon was much like today's BB gun, but more powerful. He would amaze the Indian tribes with its power and accuracy.

Lewis bought compasses, a telescope, two sextants, and a chronometer, used to make accurate readings of the expedition's

A reproduction of the compass used by William Clark to collect daily readings of distance and direction. He used these readings to draw a map of the West for President Jefferson. Today the original compass is in the Smithsonian Institute in Washington, D.C.

Lewis & Clark: Adventures West

longitude. He also purchased other supplies, like tent cloth, pliers, chisels, saws and hatchets, fishing hooks, 12 pounds (5 kg) of soap, 45 flannel shirts, shoes, woolen pants, blankets, knives, 500 rifle flints, and lead to make bullets.

Lewis also bought presents to give to the Native Americans they expected to meet. The gifts included mirrors, sewing needles, bright-colored cloth, colored beads, tobacco, and bright red vermilion, which was prized for making face paint.

Lewis also purchased medical supplies, including 600 "Rush's Thunderbolts," powerful laxative cure-alls. Dr. Rush was convinced that by inducing severe diarrhea, a patient could expel toxins that caused illness. As historian Stephen Ambrose noted, it was exactly the wrong treatment to give a sick person, but it sure kept the men's insides cleaned out.

By the time he was finished, Lewis had bought over 3,500 pounds (1,588 kg) of supplies. But he knew he needed something else: a co-commander to help lead the expedition. He also knew just the man for the job.

WELL ARMED

The Corps of Discovery went into the West armed with the most powerful weapons of the time, including the Model 1803 (above), the U.S. Army's first standard-issue rifle. The .54-caliber Model 1803 was a muzzle-loading flintlock, with a 33-inch (84-cm) barrel. It could be fired twice a minute, and take down a deer at 100 yards (91 m). Captain Lewis bought 15 of these advanced weapons at the United States Armory at Harpers Ferry.

Some of the men of the Corps of Discovery carried their own civilian rifles, usually "Kentucky" or "Pennsylvania" long rifles. The captains also carried pistols.

Mounted on the front of the expedition's keelboat was a small cannon, called a swivel gun, which could quickly pivot and shoot a one-pound (.45-kg) iron ball. The keelboat and the pirogues were also armed with bell-mouthed blunderbusses, which could fire buckshot in any direction.

June 19, 1803
Dear Clark,

My friend . . . If there is anything in this enterprise, which would induce you to participate with me in it's fatiegues, it's dangers and it's honors, believe me there is no man on earth with whom I should feel equal pleasure in sharing them as with yourself.

MERIWETHER LEWIS

July 17, 1803
Dear Lewis,

This is an undertaking fraited with many dificulties, but My friend I do assure you that no man lives whith whome I would perfur to undertake Such a Trip.

WILLIAM CLARK

William Clark

fter buying supplies, Lewis prepared to return to Washington. By this time, he had decided he needed a co-commander: his old army buddy William Clark. Maybe Lewis felt a little overwhelmed at the task he was taking on. Perhaps he realized, given his bouts of depression, that he needed help directing the men of the Corps. Or maybe Lewis simply wanted a friend for the long trip to come. Whatever the reason, Lewis wrote to Clark, inviting him to join the Corps of Discovery.

William Clark, although born in Virginia, had spent most of his life on the wild frontiers of Kentucky and Ohio, learning to fight and negotiate with Native Americans. Like Lewis, he was a seasoned woodsman. A former army captain, Clark had once been Lewis's commander. They had known each other for only six months, but in that time had grown to be great friends.

Clark, a sturdy man, with flaming red hair, was four years older than Lewis. He wasn't as educated, but had more practical experience in the military. He had a steady personality. He was outgoing and confident, an inspired leader of men. Where Lewis might get upset about a situation, Clark would remain calm and think his way out of the problem. Their skills complemented each other, and they trusted one another completely.

In a letter to Clark, Lewis broke with military tradition and asked his friend to be co-commander of the expedition. Lewis promised Clark that they would share the rank of captain. Clark quickly accepted the offer.

In the military, it's very unusual to split command. The army refused to go along with the scheme. When Clark's commission finally arrived, it was as a second lieutenant, not captain. Lewis was embarrassed. He insisted that he and Clark keep the matter a secret, and always referred to Clark as captain. They would be equals throughout the expedition.

William Clark, painted by Charles Willson Peale.

*The sale assures forever the power of the United States, and
I have given England a rival who, sooner or later, will humble
her pride.*

NAPOLÉON BONAPARTE, 1803
COMMENTING ON THE LOUISIANA PURCHASE

INTO THE UNKNOWN

In late summer 1803, Lewis had a 55-foot (17-m) keelboat made near Pittsburgh, Pennsylvania, on the Ohio River. From there he planned to float the expedition's supplies down the Ohio, picking up Clark along the way. They were heading to St. Louis, where the Corps would spend the winter of 1803-04. On the way, Lewis and Clark would handpick the best men available to join the expedition. They would come from all walks of life. Most had military experience, but many were civilians, including hunters, plus French trappers to row the pair of boats, called pirogues, that would follow alongside the keelboat.

Just before Lewis left Washington to head west, something unexpected happened. It would have a huge impact on the Corps of Discovery's mission.

William Clark's map of the Great Falls of the Columbia River.

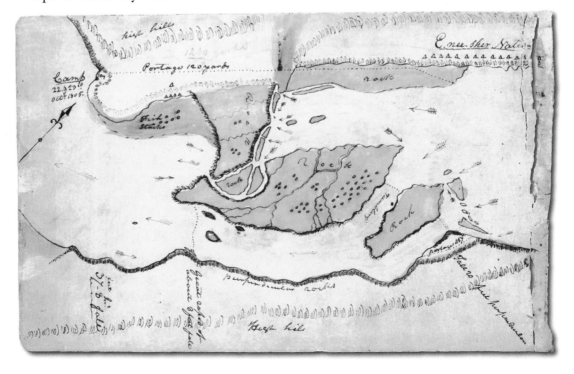

Artist Bob Scriver sculpted this statue of Meriwether Lewis, William Clark, and Sacagawea, the young Indian woman who joined the expedition during their winter stay at the Mandan villages in present-day North Dakota. The statue is located in Fort Benton, Montana, overlooking the Missouri River.

One year earlier, in 1802, President Jefferson had sent diplomats to France. He wanted to buy New Orleans, an important French-controlled port at the mouth of the Mississippi River. Whoever controlled New Orleans controlled river traffic on the Mississippi. If the United States wanted to expand westward and set up trade, it needed free access to the Mississippi. There were only a few roads back then; rivers were the superhighways of the time.

Instead of selling New Orleans to the Americans, French ruler Napoléon Bonaparte made a counteroffer: he would sell the entire French-controlled Louisiana Territory, all 820,000 square miles (2,123,798 sq. km) of it. France was at war with England, and badly needed money. The $15 million Napoléon wanted for Louisiana would help the war effort. He also knew that he could never put enough soldiers in Louisiana to stop the westward migration of American settlers. He would lose the territory anyway.

President Jefferson jumped at the chance to buy Louisiana, paying a mere 3-cents per acre for the land. With one deal he nearly doubled the size of the United States.

Napoléon declared that by selling the entire Louisiana Territory, he had "strengthened forever" the United States. "I have just given to England," he said, "a rival that will sooner or later humble her pride."

Not everybody liked the purchase, however. Jefferson's political enemies thought it was a horrible waste of money ($15 million was almost twice the federal budget at the time). Why on earth, they asked, did the United States need any more land? Didn't it have enough already? The Boston *Columbian Centinel* wrote, "A great waste, a wilderness unpeopled with any beings except wolves and wandering Indians. We are to give money of which we have too little, for land of which we already have too much."

But Jefferson was sure the Louisiana Purchase would greatly strengthen the young nation. He was one step closer to realizing his dream of spreading democracy from coast to coast. The Corps of Discovery would now be exploring American territory.

On July 4, 1803, the news of the purchase was announced. The trouble was, most of the map of Louisiana Territory was a big blank. What was out there? Were there really woolly mammoths, erupting volcanoes, and mountains of pure salt, as Jefferson's books foretold? Louisiana Territory was a huge unknown, a true mystery.

The next day Meriwether Lewis left Washington, D.C., for St. Louis. The Corps of Discovery was on its way. Lewis and Clark would soon see for themselves what lay in that vast, unexplored land.

A thunderstorm produces a rainbow on the plains of Montana near the Rocky Mountains.

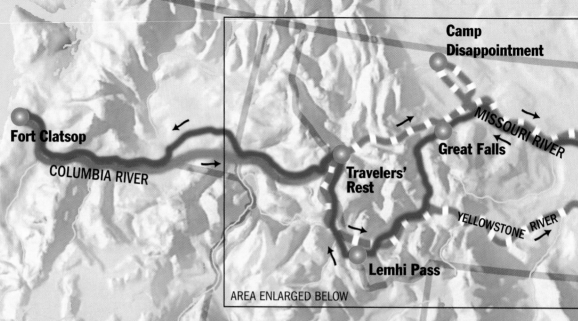

Camp
Disappointment

MISSOURI RIVER

Great Falls

Travelers'
Rest

YELLOWSTONE RIVER

Lemhi Pass

Fort Clatsop

COLUMBIA RIVER

AREA ENLARGED BELOW

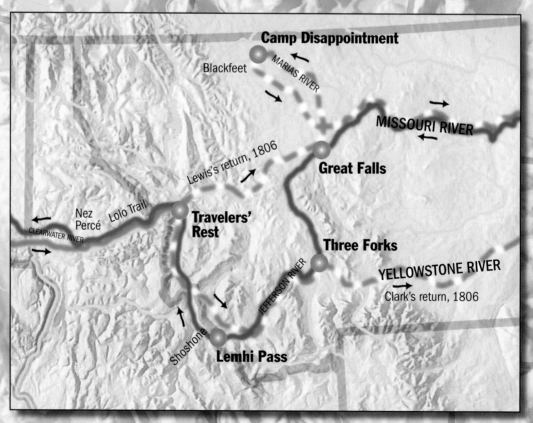

Camp Disappointment

Blackfeet

MARIAS RIVER

MISSOURI RIVER

Lewis's return, 1806

Great Falls

Nez
Percé

Lolo Trail

CLEARWATER RIVER

Travelers'
Rest

Three Forks

JEFFERSON RIVER

YELLOWSTONE RIVER

Clark's return, 1806

Shoshone

Lemhi Pass

Fort Mandan

Teton Sioux

MISSOURI RIVER

Yankton
Sioux

Floyd's
Grave

Camp
Dubois

St. Louis

Meriwether Lewis   William Clark

LEGEND

Westbound route, 1804-1805

Return route, 1806

Lewis & Clark separate routes, 1806

LEWIS & CLARK
ADVENTURES
WEST

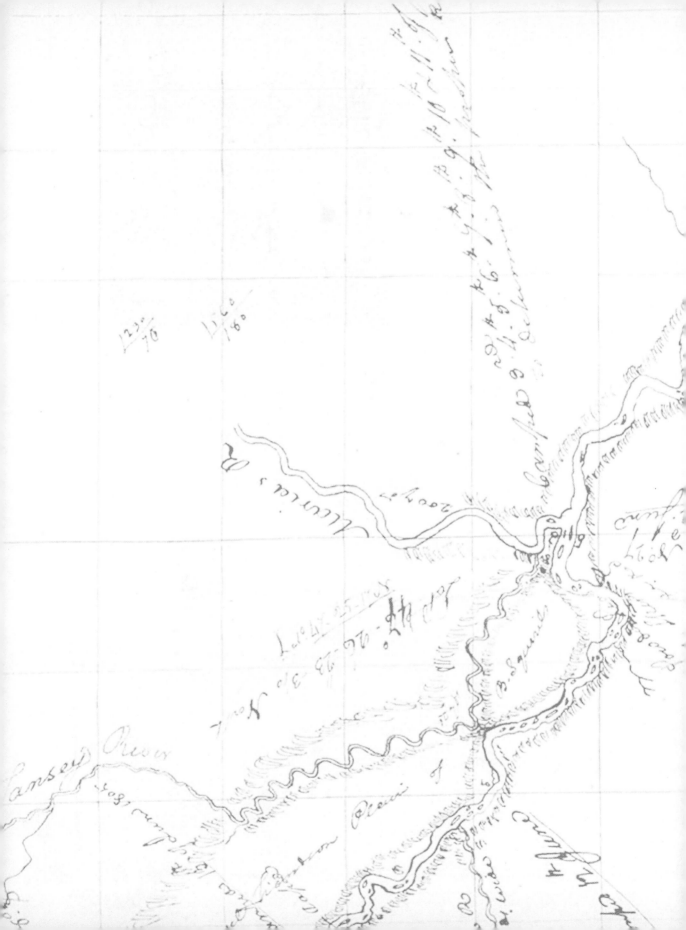

PART TWO
UP THE MISSOURI

Dear Captain Lewis,
*   The acquisition of the country through*
which you are to pass has inspired the
public generally with a great deal of
interest in your enterprize. . . . Present my
salutations to Mr. Clarke, assure all your
party that we have our eyes turned on them
with anxiety for their safety.

THOMAS JEFFERSON
JANUARY, 1804

MAKE READY

On July 5, 1803, Meriwether Lewis left Washington, D.C. Near Pittsburgh he had a large keelboat built to carry men and cargo. When it was finished, Lewis sailed down the Ohio River, picking up William Clark and eager recruits along the way to St. Louis.

By December 1803, Lewis and Clark set up camp on the Illinois side of the Mississippi River, just upstream from St. Louis. On the opposite shore, the Missouri River emptied into the Mississippi. The explorers constructed several huts, which they called Camp Dubois (also called Camp Wood). When the camp was finished, they settled in for the winter to collect supplies and train their men for the journey to come.

In the winter, the Corps could not travel. The snow was too deep, it was too cold, and there wasn't enough game to hunt. After settling in at Camp Dubois to wait out the winter of 1803-1804, Clark began training the men. Most were soldiers, since this was to be a military expedition. Finding volunteers was no problem. With the added promise of money and land, the expedition would be the trip of a lifetime.

The men came from all corners of the United States, and from all walks of life. Lewis wrote that they were looking for "Stout, healthy, unmarried men, accustomed to the woods, and capable of bearing bodily fatigue."

Fresh meat roasts over an open campfire at a reenactment in Great Falls, Montana. To keep their energy levels up, the men of the Corps ate up to nine pounds (four kg) of meat each day.

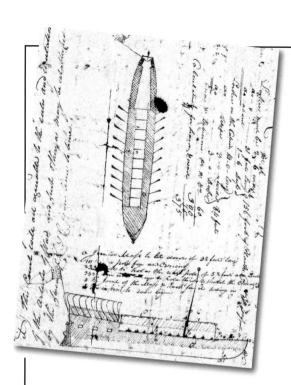

THE KEELBOAT

Keelboats are large, flat-bottomed freight boats once common on the Mississippi and Missouri Rivers. Clark's journal at left shows the expedition's keelboat. It was 55 feet (16.8 m) long, and 8 feet (2.4 m) wide. The stern (back) held a small cabin with windows, with a deck on top. The bow had a small cannon, or swivel gun, which could quickly be turned in any direction.

The center of the keelboat was the cargo area, which held 10 tons (9 metric tons) of supplies. More cargo was held in lockers along the sides of the boat. These had wooden lids that could be raised to protect the men if they were attacked.

Twenty oars powered the keelboat. It also had a mast, on which two sails could be raised if the wind was at the explorers' backs. The Missouri River was sometimes too shallow to row such a big boat. Men with long poles pushed against the river bottom and walked toward the back of the boat, inching the vessel forward. Sometimes even this didn't work, and the men had to resort to *cordelling* (core-delling), trudging on shore and pulling the boat with heavy ropes.

Charles Floyd was a 22-year-old soldier from Kentucky. "A young man of much merit," Lewis wrote. Floyd and Nathanial Pryor were cousins. Reubin and Joseph Field were brothers. John Ordway was a young man from Hebron, New Hampshire. John Shields, the oldest enlisted man, at 35, was an expert blacksmith. Joseph Whitehouse was a tailor from Virginia, Patrick Gass a carpenter from Pennsylvania. The youngest man was George Shannon, who turned 19 in 1804.

William Clark brought along a man named York. He was an African-American slave who had been with Clark since childhood. During the journey, the big man would prove his worth many times, becoming an important part of the Corps.

Lewis & Clark: Adventures West

Lewis also brought a Newfoundland dog, called Seaman. The dog, who weighed nearly 150 pounds (68 kg), helped hunt and guard the camp. Seaman was quick to fetch squirrels, geese, and beaver for his master. He once ran down a deer that had been wounded by a hunter. Even more impressively, on May 29, 1805, while the Corps was in present-day Montana, Seaman chased off a buffalo that had wandered into camp in the middle of the night and threatened to trample a group of sleeping men.

The Corps employed several civilians. George Drouillard (pronounced *Drew-yer*) was the son of a French-Canadian father and Shawnee Indian mother. He was a skilled hunter, knew the lower Missouri River, and could speak the sign language of the Plains Indians.

Clark drilled the volunteers during their five-month stay at Camp Dubois. He prepared them to work as a team. He carefully noted who best followed orders, who was strongest, quickest, who had the most endurance. He looked for good carpentry and metalworking skills, and noted who were the best hunters.

Lewis, meanwhile, spent time across the river in St. Louis gathering last-minute supplies. In 1803, St. Louis was a frontier town with less than 1,500 people. Lewis questioned trappers and explorers who had ventured partway up the Missouri. He learned enough to have a rough idea of what they would find, at least until they reached the Mandan Indian villages of present-day North Dakota. Beyond that point, no American citizen had ever ventured.

Camp Dubois, on the Illinois side of the Mississippi River. Because the river channel has shifted over the years, it is only an approximate location of the Corps' winter quarters of 1803-04.

Monday 14th May 1804 hard Showers of rain. This being the day appointed by Capt. Clark to Set out . . . we fired our Swivel on the bow hoisted Sail and Set out in high Spirits for the western Expedition.

JOSEPH WHITEHOUSE

UNDERWAY

On May 14, 1804, the Corps of Discovery—nearly four-dozen strong—set off from Camp Dubois. The keelboat and two canoe-like pirogues, one red, one white, crossed the Mississippi—"Under a jentle brease," wrote William Clark—and entered the mouth of the Missouri River. With Clark on deck, they finally left their dreary winter quarters behind and started the expedition for which they had waited so long.

Clark was in a cheerful mood. Below him on the main deck, 20 men strained in unison at their oars, rowing against the muddy current of the Missouri. They traveled four and a half miles (seven km) that first day, stopping on an island to camp. Two days later they made it to the small French town of St. Charles. Meriwether Lewis, who had been in St. Louis picking up last-minute supplies, hurried his horse through a fierce thunderstorm to meet the expedition. The citizens of St. Charles threw a festive ball in honor of the Corps. After being cooped up in winter camp for so long, the men were happy to relax and have some fun.

On May 25, they passed La Charette, an outpost of seven small huts. Sergeant Charles Floyd wrote in his journal that it was "the last settlement of whites on this river." They were now beyond the reaches of Western civilization.

This early painting by Charles A. Morganthaler shows the Corps as it departs from St. Charles. The keelboat is incorrectly shown with a front cabin.

A replica of Lewis's iron-framed canoe, which the men called "The Experiment." Lewis planned for it to be carried until needed, then covered with hides and sealed with pine pitch. Pine trees proved scarce in present-day Montana, and the boat had to be abandoned at the Great Falls.

The landscape of the lower Missouri River was beautiful to behold, with wildflowers and fruit trees dotting the shoreline. Forested limestone bluffs rose up on either side, covered with hardwood trees in full spring bloom. Ducks, wild birds, and frogs added a chorus of song to the humid air.

Travel up the river was slow. Today, dams have tamed the Missouri. In 1804 the river was still wild. Currents were unpredictable. Churning, muddy water hid rocks and sandbars. Fallen trees, called snags, were swept downriver, sometimes lurking just under the brown water. Maneuvering the huge keelboat was always a challenge. Once it got hung up on a snag and nearly overturned.

The Missouri River was very swift. The men had to row five miles per hour (eight km/h) just to stay even with the current. They avoided the main channel, shifting from eddy to eddy, looking for relatively still water. Sometimes overhanging trees along the shore snagged the keelboat's mast, snapping it in two.

On a good day, the expedition made 14 miles (23 km). When the wind was at their backs, they could hoist sails and get a boost. More often, though, they had to use poles to push against the river bottom, or pull the boats by rope, either in the shallows or along the banks. It was backbreaking work. Thunderstorms often forced them to stop. After two months, they were still in what is now the state of Missouri.

A reenactor portraying George Drouillard, hired by Lewis and Clark as a hunter and Native American interpreter.

Tuesday 29ᵗʰ May. Rained last night, the river rises fast.
The Musquetors are verry bad.

WILLIAM CLARK, 1804

WE PROCEEDED ON

As the Corps of Discovery made its way up the Missouri River, some men rowed or pulled the boats. Others hunted for game along the shore. The men used so much energy rowing and pulling that they ate seven to nine pounds (3 to 4 kg) of meat each day just to keep their strength up. The expedition's best hunter was George Drouillard, who was an expert marksman. Lewis wrote in his journals, "I scarcely know how we should subsist were it not for the exertions of this excellent hunter."

William Clark spent most of his time on the keelboat, taking compass readings and measuring distances for a map he would later draw for Thomas Jefferson.

Lewis often walked or rode his horse on shore, helping hunt game or making notes about the plants and animals they saw. Soon after leaving St. Charles, Lewis climbed a limestone cliff. He slipped and almost fell 300 feet (91 m) to his death. Clark wrote that Lewis "Saved himself by the assistance of his Knife . . . he caught at 20 foot."

A man stands at the helm of a replica of the keelboat. Two blunderbusses are mounted on each side of the deck.

47

THE JOURNALS

One of the reasons we know so much about the Corps of Discovery is that Lewis and Clark kept daily journals. The captains recorded each day's events in their elkskin-covered notebooks, noting the plants and animals they came across, the weather, American Indians they encountered, and anything else "worthy of notice." Lewis and Clark insisted that other men of the Corps keep journals also, in case the captains' journals were lost or damaged. Patrick Gass, Charles Floyd, John Ordway, and Joseph Whitehouse were among those who kept their own journals. Their notes help fill in the gaps of the captains' journals, giving us a more complete picture of the expedition.

Something you might notice when reading the journals are the misspelled words. Back in those days, there was no standardized spelling—it would be another 24 years before Noah Webster published his first dictionary. Journal writers simply wrote phonetically, spelling words as they thought they should be sounded out. For example, the word *mosquito* appears in the journals in many different ways, including musquetor, musqutor, musquitoe, misquetor, musquetoe, musquitoe, and musketoe.

Insects were a constant misery. Armies of ticks dug into the men's flesh, and mosquitoes swarmed around their faces. Lewis wrote that mosquitoes were "so numerous that we frequently get them in our throats as we breathe." The men smeared bear grease on their bodies to keep the pests at bay. At night they used mosquito netting that Lewis had brought.

In the evening, the Corps broke up into three squads, each led by its own sergeant. Each squad did its own cooking, cleaning, and repairing of equipment. Evening also gave them a chance to rest their weary bodies. Many of the men got sick, or had bad shoulders and joints. Some suffered from snakebite. Their drinking water came from the muddy Missouri, which gave them diarrhea. Lewis tended to the men with his knowledge of medicine and herbal healing.

The journey was difficult, but the men were young and tough, and their spirits remained high. They marked the first Fourth of July ever celebrated west of the Mississippi River by firing the keelboat's cannon.

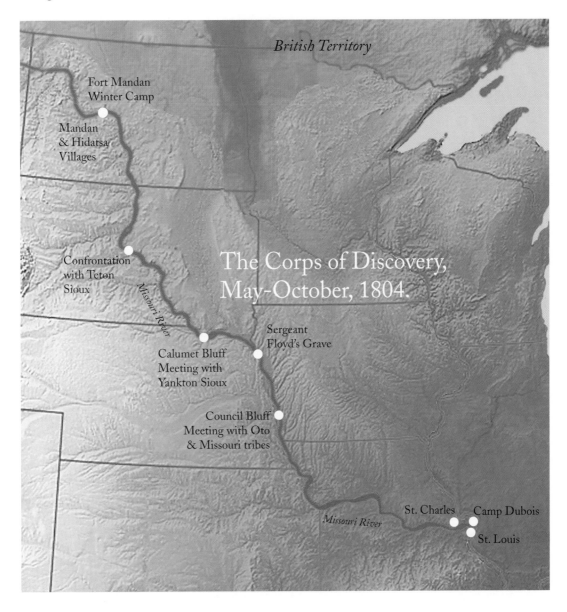

The Corps of Discovery, May-October, 1804.

The best authenticated accounts informed
us, that we were to pass through a country
possessed by numerous, powerful and
warlike nations of savages, of gigantic
stature, fierce, treacherous and cruel; and
particularly hostile to white men.

PATRICK GASS

My heart is gladder than it ever was before
to see [a white man]. If you want
to open the road, no one can prevent it.
It will always be open to you.

KAKAWISSASSA,
LIGHTNING CROW

THE PRAIRIE TRIBES

*L*ewis and Clark were under orders by Thomas Jefferson to contact as many Native American tribes as possible. Jefferson was especially interested in setting up fur-trading partnerships. He knew that trade and commerce would encourage people to settle into the new territories, expanding the reach of the United States.

Jefferson also had a scientific curiosity about Native Americans. He ordered Lewis and Clark to study their language, culture, and customs.

During the first part of their journey, there were few Indian encounters. The tribes were out on the Great Plains, hunting buffalo. Finally, on August 3, 1804, the Corps had its first meeting with western Indians near present-day Omaha, Nebraska. They met for a day with members of the Oto and Missouri Indian tribes at a place Clark called "Council Bluff."

Painted lodges of the Plains Indians, photographed by Edward S. Curtis.

Lewis and Clark had a routine for meeting with the Native Americans. Dressed in their finest uniforms and three-cornered hats, they first told the Indians that they had a new "White Father" (Thomas Jefferson). Then they displayed modern technology, such as rifles, magnets, and spyglasses. The men paraded and marched in military formation, firing volleys from their rifles. Lewis demonstrated his specially built air rifle, which greatly impressed the Indians.

They handed out presents, representing the wealth of the United States. The gifts included beads, flags, vermilion, knives, tobacco, and special peace medals for the Indian chiefs. The medals had a portrait of Thomas Jefferson engraved on one side, and two hands clasped in friendship on the other.

Lastly, Lewis and Clark urged the Indians to stop making war against their neighbors, and to make the United States their trade partner. They promised peace and prosperity if they did as they were told.

White people had been trading on the lower Missouri for nearly a century before Lewis and Clark passed through. The Native Americans had heard this kind of arrogant talk before. It was very insulting to be told that the land they had occupied for generations was suddenly "owned" by an unseen "White Father" in the East.

Still, most of the Indians who encountered Lewis and Clark on the Missouri were eager to start a trade partnership with the Americans. They wanted metal tools to make their lives easier, and they wanted weapons to give them an advantage over their neighbors.

The front and back of the peace medals Lewis and Clark gave to Native American chiefs.

Plains Indians photographed by Edward S. Curtis 100 years after the Lewis and Clark expedition.

A George Catlin painting of a Plains Indian hunting buffalo.

20ᵗʰ August. Sergeant Floyd much weaker and no better.... No pulse & nothing will Stay a moment on his Stomach.... Passed two Islands ... and at the first Bluff on the [starboard side] Serj. Floyd Died with a great deal of composure, before his death he Said to me, "I am going away. I want you to write me a letter."

WILLIAM CLARK

On August 20, 1804, near present-day Sioux City, Iowa, Sergeant Charles Floyd died. Lewis wrote that he passed away from "bilious cholic." Historians think Floyd probably suffered a burst appendix. Even if he had been safely back home, nothing could have saved him—doctors didn't yet know how to perform appendectomies.

Floyd was buried on a bluff overlooking the Missouri River. His grave is marked today by a giant stone monument. Floyd was the first U.S. soldier to die west of the Mississippi River, and would be the only fatality of the Corps of Discovery.

On August 30, the Corps met with a group of friendly Yankton Sioux Indians at a place called Calumet Bluff. Clark, who was always more at ease among the Native Americans than Lewis, called the Yanktons a "stout, bold looking people."

The meeting was a success: the Yankton chiefs agreed to more trade with the Americans. One chief even agreed to travel east to meet with President Jefferson.

But the chiefs had a warning for Lewis and Clark. Chief Half Man told them that the next tribe upriver would not be so friendly. These, the chief said, were the powerful and feared Teton Sioux, the Lakotas, and they "will not open their ears, and you cannot, I fear, open them."

There is no timber in this part of the country; but continued prairie on both sides of the river. A person by going on one of the hills may have a view as far as the eye can reach without any obstruction; and enjoy the most delightful prospects.

PATRICK GASS

THE GREAT PLAINS

By September of 1804, the Corps had moved onto the Great Plains, the largest grassland of the world. The only trees hugged the river bottom; beyond that, there was nothing but grassland, rolling hills that stretched to the horizon.

The men could see vast herds of wildlife—elk, deer, and buffalo by the thousands. There were wolves and owls, ducks and frogs, hawks and grouse. The immense open Plains stunned the explorers. It was like a vast Garden of Eden. It was especially surprising because they had lived their whole lives in wooded areas. A common saying at the time was that a squirrel could jump from tree to tree all the way to the Mississippi River. At the Great Plains, the squirrel stopped.

Lewis and Clark began cataloguing plants and animals that were unknown back home, and new to science: coyotes, mule deer, jackrabbits. They were the first to describe pronghorn, the fastest animal in North America, clocked at over 70 miles per hour (113 kmph). Native Americans knew these animals, of course, and fur trappers had seen them before. But the journals of Lewis and Clark were the first detailed descriptions of these "curiousities," as the captains called them.

Pronghorn grazing on the plains of South Dakota.

Prairie dogs on the plains of North Dakota.

I have called [it] the barking squirrel.... It's form is that of the squirrel ... [but] they bark at you as you approach them, their note being much that of little toy dogs.... It is much more quick active and fleet than it's form would indicate.

MERIWETHER LEWIS

On September 7, the Corps discovered "barking squirrels," or as John Ordway called them, prairie dogs. The entire expedition struggled for hours to capture one. They finally succeeded by pouring water down its hole and flushing it out. The prairie dog was caged and eventually sent back live to a delighted President Jefferson, along with several boxes of skins and plant specimens.

In late August Private George Shannon, the youngest member of the Corps at 19, got lost while hunting on the Plains. He made it back to the river, but found nobody there. He thought the expedition had left without him, so he hurried upstream, trying to catch up. Actually, the rest of the men were *behind* Shannon!

After two weeks on his own, the lost teenager finally sat down on the riverbank. His only hope was that a fur-trading boat might someday pick him up. The Corps eventually caught up to Shannon and found him there, starving and weak. He had run out of bullets, living on nothing but a rabbit and some wild grapes.

Clark later wrote in his journal, "Thus a man had like to have Starved to death in a land of Plenty for the want of Bullitts or Something to kill his meat."

A snake hunts for food on the bluffs overlooking the Missouri River in North Dakota.

You will probably meet with parties of [the Teton Sioux]. On that nation we wish most particularly to make a friendly impression, because of their immense power.

THOMAS JEFFERSON

CLOSE CALL

On September 25, 1804, the Corps of Discovery finally encountered a band of Teton Sioux—the Lakotas—at the mouth of the Bad River, near today's Pierre, South Dakota. The Lakotas were a powerful group, and hostile to their neighbors and the few whites who traveled through their territory. Fur trappers called them the bullies of the Missouri River.

Lewis and Clark gave their usual Indian speech and demonstration, but their audience was unimpressed. The Lakotas controlled river traffic and the trade of their neighbors. The Corps of Discovery's mission threatened to distrupt their monopoly on trade. It threatened their way of life.

The Lakotas demanded more gifts. They also told the Corps that they would not be allowed to travel any farther upriver. Lewis and Clark arranged for three of the Teton Sioux chiefs to tour the expedition's keelboat. After the tour, the chiefs were still hostile, so Clark took them back to shore in one of the pirogues. Then things got ugly.

Warriors grabbed the pirogue's towrope. One of the chiefs got into a heated argument with Clark. The captain drew his sword. Warriors along the riverbank nocked their arrows, ready to fire.

The site where Lewis and Clark first met the Teton Sioux, at the confluence of the Missouri and Bad Rivers, near present-day Pierre, South Dakota.

Capt Clark Spoke to all the party to Stand to their arm. Capt Lewis who was on board [the keelboat] ordered every man to his arms. The large Swivel [gun was] loaded immediately with 16 Musquet balls in it, the 2 other Swivels loaded well with Buck Shot [and] each of them manned. Capt Clark . . . told them that we must and would go on . . . that we were not Squaws, but warriers.

The chief Sayed he had warriers too and if we were to go on they would follow us and kill and take the whole of us by degrees.

JOHN ORDWAY

It was a tense moment, one that could easily have ended in disaster, with many killed on each side. Instead, a Lakota chief, Black Buffalo, wisely defused the crisis. He changed the subject and requested only that the women and children of his village be allowed to visit the keelboat before the Corps moved on.

After three nervous days among the Lakota, the Corps departed, happy to put some distance between themselves and the "bullies of the Missouri."

In early October, the men encountered members of the Arikara tribe. They had once numbered almost 30,000, but 20 years earlier a smallpox epidemic killed nine of ten Arikaras. On October 8, the Corps met the survivors, who were much friendlier than the Teton Sioux.

Hollow Horn Bear, from the Brulé band of the Teton Sioux, photographed by Edward S. Curtis.

October 21ˢᵗ. We had a disagreeable night of sleet and hail. It snowed during the forenoon, but we proceeded early on our voyage.

SERGEANT PATRICK GASS

A Sioux council, painted by George Catlin.

The days of October shortened and grew cold. Huge flocks of birds flew overhead on their migration south. In what is now North Dakota, Clark estimated they had traveled 1,600 miles (2,575 km) up the Missouri River.

They had hoped to make it to the river's headwaters by now, but they weren't even close. With winter fast approaching, the captains knew they had to stop soon to build a fort and prepare for cold weather. They decided to stop at the Mandan Indian villages, the last known point on their maps. That spring they would venture into unknown lands. But first, they had to survive a harsh, bone-chilling winter on the Great Plains.

October 31, 1804. The river being very low and the season so far advanced that it frequently shuts up with ice in this climate we determined to spend the Winter in this neighborhood.

MERIWETHER LEWIS

Winter Among the Mandans

In September 1804, the Corps of Discovery almost fought an all-out battle with the Teton Sioux tribe near present-day Pierre, South Dakota. Skillful diplomacy by the Indian chiefs and Captains Lewis and Clark averted disaster, but tensions remained high. As they continued their way upstream along the Missouri River, the men of the expedition felt nervous about future Native Americans they were sure to meet.

Their tension was relieved in late October when they landed their boats about 50 miles (80 km) north of present-day Bismarck, North Dakota. Five Indian earth-lodge villages—two Mandan and three Hidatsa—were situated along the Missouri within a few miles of each other, close to the mouth of the Knife River. The Native Americans welcomed the expedition with open arms.

The Mandan and Hidatsa villages contained about 4,500 people, more than the population of Washington, D.C., at the time. They were successful farmers, living in one place, unlike their nomadic neighbors the Sioux. Instead of portable tepees, they built permanent earth lodges. Although they were farmers, the Mandans and Hidatsas were also skilled buffalo hunters. They depended on the great herds for meat and hides.

The Knife River settlements were the center of a huge Great Plains trading network. Neighboring tribes, including Crow, Assiniboine, Cheyenne, Cree, and Lakota Indians, traded for corn raised by the Mandans and Hidatsas, in exchange for horses, buffalo hides, and weapons.

Above: A Karl Bodmer painting of Mandan chief Mato-Tope.
Far left: The inside of a Hidatsa earth lodge in present-day North Dakota.
Below: The frozen Missouri River on a January morning in North Dakota.

The Mandan and Hidatsa tribes had done business with British, French, and Spanish traders for 70 years before the Corps of Discovery arrived. British fur traders regularly visited the villages. The tribes were used to dealing with white people, unlike the more suspicious Teton Sioux.

The Mandan Indians were especially eager to set up a trading partnership with the Americans. They wanted to trade for tools that would make their lives easier, like metal goods and rifles. With the help of translator René Jessaume, a French-Canadian fur trapper who had lived with the Mandans for 15 years, Lewis and Clark soon made friends with the Native Americans. Their strongest allies were Mandan chiefs Black Cat and Sheheke (whom Lewis and Clark called Big White), and a Hidatsa chief named Black Moccasin.

Above: Hidatsa chief Black Moccasin, by George Catlin.

Our wish is to be at peace with all. . . . If we eat, you shall eat; if we starve, you must starve also.

SHEHEKE, BIG WHITE

Above: Karl Bodmer's 1834-35 painting of Mandan Indians crossing the frozen Missouri River. The Corps of Discovery passed through the area years earlier. Fort Clark is in the background, next to a Mandan village.

Left: Reenactor Mike Scholl stands at the entrance of a replica of Fort Mandan, built near the original site in present-day North Dakota. The morning this photo was taken, the temperature sank to minus 12 degrees Fahrenheit (-24 C), typical weather for the Corps during the winter of 1804-1805.

Winter Among the Mandans

Big Medicine, by Charles M. Russell. A Hidatsa chief spit on his finger and rubbed it on York's skin. He wanted to be sure York wasn't a painted white man. York was the first African-American the Mandans had ever seen.

With bone-chilling weather quickly approaching, Lewis and Clark decided to stop for the winter. Clark estimated they had traveled 1,600 miles (2,575 km) from St. Louis, but there was still a long way to go before they reached the headwaters of the Missouri River.

Lewis ordered his men to build a wooden fort along the banks of the river, directly across from one of the Mandan villages. There were enough trees there for firewood, and to build their triangular-shaped stockade. Fort Mandan, as Lewis and Clark called it, had walls 18 feet (5.5 m) high, with eight huts inside for sleeping quarters, a guardroom, a blacksmith shop, and storehouses.

The days grew shorter as winter crept up upon the wind-swept Great Plains. By mid-November, ice was flowing on the river. The thermometer sank lower and lower, dipping to 45 degrees below zero (-43 C) on the night of December 17. Sergeant John Ordway wrote that it was "colder than I ever knew it to be in the States." Most of the men suffered from frostbite. Sometimes the temperature dropped so low that

A sketch from Meriwether Lewis's journal showing the design of the battle ax the Corps bartered to the Mandans for corn.

water trapped inside cottonwood trees expanded, shattering the trunks with an ear-deafening sound, like a cannon being shot off.

December 12th. Clear and cold.... It is Several degrees colder this morning than it has been before, so that we did nothing but git wood for our fires. Our Rooms are verry close and warm, So we can keep ourselves warm and comfortable, but the Sentinel who Stood out in the open weather had to be relieved every hour all day.

JOHN ORDWAY

By Christmas Eve 1804, Fort Mandan was officially completed. On New Year's Day, the men celebrated with their Native American neighbors. The Indians were delighted by the fiddle playing of one-eyed Pierre Cruzatte, and by the lively dancing of the other men. They were especially amazed at Captain Clark's slave, York. He was a big, athletic man, but the Mandans were more intrigued by his dark skin, having never before seen an African-American.

Karl Bodmer's *The Bison Dance of the Mandan Indians.* During the winter of 1804-1805, the Mandans invited the men of the Corps to take part in this sacred ritual, which the Indians believed called the buffalo herds back to the land near the Mandan villages.

An Edward S. Paxson painting of Sacagawea. She, and her husband and baby, slept in the same tent as Lewis and Clark for much of the journey.

Indians often walked across the frozen Missouri to visit or trade. Lewis and Clark kept an open-door policy at the fort. They wanted to learn as much as they could about Native American customs and beliefs. They also traded for food, which was in short supply at the fort as winter dragged on. If it hadn't been for the Indians, the Corps might have starved to death that cold winter.

In exchange for Mandan corn, Privates John Shields and Alexander Willard provided blacksmithing services. Their metal battle ax heads were in high demand. In fact, they were so popular that later that next summer, after crossing the Rocky Mountains, the Corps would discover Nez Percé Indians using the battle axes. The trading network of the Native American tribes was much bigger than Lewis and Clark first imagined.

In addition to providing corn, the Mandans invited the men of the Corps to join them on buffalo hunts. The Americans were amazed at the skill of their Indian hosts. The Mandans rode bareback at breakneck speed, steering their ponies with their knees as they leaned over and shot arrows into the fleeing buffaloes. Indian women quickly butchered the carcasses on the spot before hungry wolves could steal the meat.

Captain Lewis was busy that winter providing medical services, both to his own men, and to the Mandans in exchange for food. Once, he had to amputate the frostbitten toes of a Mandan boy, without the use of anesthesia or a bone saw.

On the freezing cold night of February 11, 1805, Lewis helped a young woman who was having trouble delivering her baby. Her name was Sacagawea. She was a Shoshone girl, who's name meant "Bird Woman." She was barely 17 years old.

Five years earlier, in the foothills of the Rocky Mountains, Sacagawea was kidnapped by a Hidatsa war party. They took her back to the Hidatsa-Mandan villages, then sold her as a slave to Toussaint Charbonneau, a French-Canadian trapper who lived among the Hidatsas. Charbonneau claimed the teenager as his wife, along with another Shoshone woman.

Lewis and Clark knew that the Shoshone Indians lived at the headwaters of the Missouri River, and that they owned ponies. The Corps would need those ponies to haul their men and equipment over the rugged Bitterroot Mountains to the Columbia River system, which flowed west to the Pacific Ocean.

Sacagawea spoke both Shoshone and Hidatsa. Her husband spoke Hidatsa and French. Lewis and Clark hired Charbonneau, knowing that he and Sacagawea could act as an interpreting team. Sacagawea could talk to her people and barter for ponies, then translate into Hidatsa for her husband. Charbonneau would then speak in French to Francois Labiche, a member of the Corps who spoke both French and English. Finally, Labiche would relay messages to the captains. It was a complicated scheme, but Lewis felt confidant it would work.

On that cold winter night in February, Sacagawea was having a long and painful labor. Somebody told Lewis that the rings of a rattlesnake, crushed into a powder and given with water, sometimes eased labor pains. Lewis found a rattlesnake from his collection of animal skins and mixed the concoction.

An Indian baby in a cradleboard, much like the kind in which Sacagawea carried her son Jean Baptiste during the expedition west. Her boy was barely two months old when they began the journey.

Whether this medicine was truly the cause or not I shall not undertake to determine, but . . . she had not taken it more than ten minutes before she brought forth. Perhaps this remedy may be worthy of future experiments.

MERIWETHER LEWIS

Sacagawea gave birth to a baby boy. Charbonneau named him Jean Baptiste. Captain Clark affectionately nicknamed him "Pomp," or "Pompy." That spring, little Pomp would become the youngest member of the Corps of Discovery.

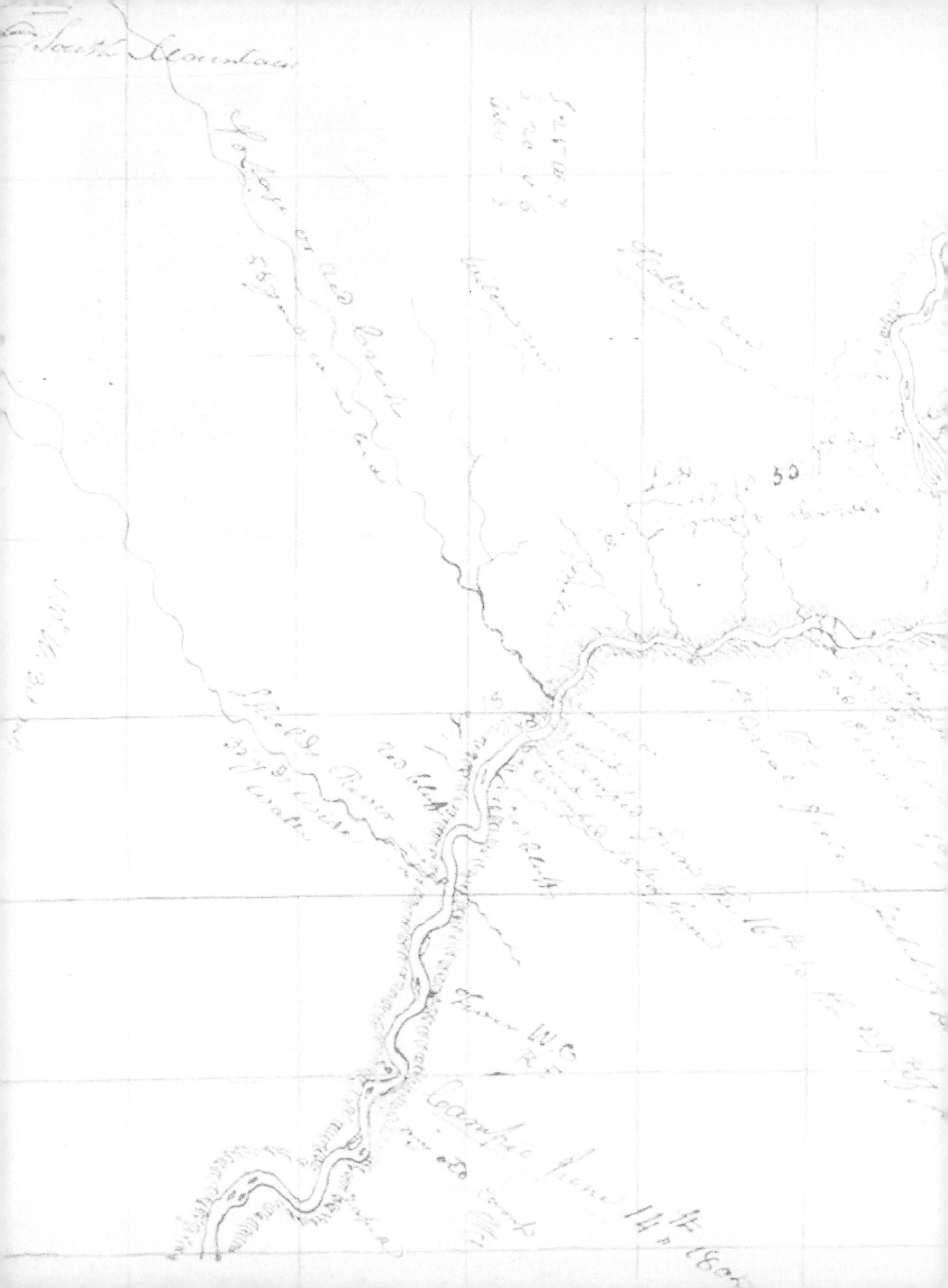

South Mountain

Shelby River

Camped June 14th 1800

PART THREE
UNCHARTED LANDS

OFF THE MAP

By March of 1805, ice on the Missouri River began breaking up. After five long months in the Mandan villages, the men of the Corps of Discovery were eager to get moving again.

Lewis and Clark sent several men back to St. Louis in the big keelboat, commanded by Corporal Richard Warfington. Captain Lewis ordered Warfington to be on alert, especially while passing through Sioux territory, to shoot his way through if necessary. The keelboat was loaded with precious cargo: animal, mineral, and plant specimens; letters; journals; maps; and progress reports of their journey so far. A magpie and a prairie dog, captured the previous summer, would make it back alive, much to the delight of President Thomas Jefferson.

On April 7, the Corps had its boats in the water, packed and ready. After saying Godspeed to their comrades, the men

April 7ᵗʰ 1805. We were now about to penetrate a country at least two thousand miles in width, on which the foot of civilized man had never trodden; . . . I could but esteem this moment of [our] departure as among the most happy of my life.

MERIWETHER LEWIS

in the keelboat headed downriver, toward St. Louis. The two pirogues, along with six dugout canoes, pointed upstream. The men dipped their paddles in the chilly water of the Missouri, then dug in, propelling their craft upriver toward points unknown.

Lewis and Clark had asked the Mandan Indians what they knew of the land to the west, but the Mandans didn't travel very much. However, the Hidatsa Indians often sent war parties onto the Great Plains, sometimes as far as the Rocky Mountains. They gave Lewis and Clark valuable information about the land, major tributaries emptying into the Missouri, and a tremendous waterfall they would encounter.

The Corps of Discovery now consisted of the "permanent party," which numbered 33, including four civilians—George Drouillard, the expedition's hunter, plus Charbonneau, Sacagawea, and her baby, Jean Baptiste. They pushed into what is now Montana, traveling through country that had been explored only by Native Americans.

Cliffs rising up above the Missouri River near Fort Benton, Montana, are set aglow by evening sunlight.

Pelicans join a flock nesting near the spot where the Yellowstone River empties into the Missouri in western North Dakota.

At first the nights were cold. Some mornings ice formed on their canoe paddles. They also fought against the prairie wind, which blew sand in their faces, and made paddling hard. The sand, Lewis wrote, was "so penetrating, we are compelled to eat, drink and breathe it."

The men were astonished by the vast numbers of animals they encountered on the Plains in Montana. It was like a Garden of Eden laid out before them. Herds of buffalo, elk, and deer spread out on the Plains as far as the eye could see. Packs of wolves followed the herds, picking off the young or weak. The men saw bighorn sheep for the first time. They saw flocks of geese, swans, and cranes flying overhead. There were so many beavers that the sound of their tails slapping on the water kept Clark awake some nights.

Roasted beaver tail was a prized delicacy. The men feasted on it, along with their usual diet of buffalo meat. The men worked hard paddling, rowing, or poling the boats upriver, which increased their appetite. The hunters kept busy providing each man with up to nine pounds (four kg) of buffalo meat each day.

Some things on the Plains were not so wonderful, and were much more menacing than the ever-present mosquitoes. The Mandan and Hidatsa Indians told Lewis and Clark they would encounter bears unlike any they had seen before in the East. These bears, the Indians warned, were giant, ferocious creatures. They were the dreaded grizzly, unknown to the easterners.

On April 29, Lewis and another hunter shot their first grizzly bear. They got lucky, killing the small bear with little trouble. Lewis bragged in his journal, "The Indians may well fear this anamal, equipped as they generally are with their bows and arrows. But in the hands of skillful riflemen they are by no means as formidable or dangerous as they have been represented."

On May 5, the Corps encountered a much larger bear, so big that Lewis called it "a monster." It took 10 shots to kill it. On May 11, they fought another grizzly, bringing it down only after shooting it through the lungs and its head, twice. Lewis wrote, "These bear being so hard to die reather intimedates us all; I must confess that I do not like the gentlemen and had reather fight two Indians than one bear."

Grizzly bears nearly killed several members of the Corps.

Above: Artist John Clymer's *Hasty Retreat* shows a grizzly bear battling members of the expedition. *Below:* A reenactor shows off a replica of a rifle used by the Corps.

Grizzlies harassed the Corps throughout their passage through Montana. It usually took several men working together to kill the enraged bears. Sometimes the men had to run away or leap into the river to save themselves while their comrades reloaded their rifles. At night the grizzlies came prowling around camp. Lewis's big Newfoundland dog, Seaman, was constantly growling and barking, trying to ward off the hungry bears.

After weeks of fighting off grizzlies, the men's earlier confidence wore off. Lewis wrote, "I find that the curiossity of our party is pretty well satisfyed with rispect to this animal."

Animals weren't the only danger the men faced. One windy day, Charbonneau was in command of a pirogue. With high waves on the river, he lost control. From shore, Lewis watched in horror as water poured over the side. The boat contained scientific instruments, medicine, journals, and maps. Losing the pirogue would be a disaster.

Luckily, Pierre Cruzatte was also in the boat, and managed to help Charbonneau regain control. Sacagawea calmly saved most of the cargo.

Charbono, still crying to his god for mercy, had not yet recollected the rudder, nor could the repeated orders of the bowsman, Cruzat, bring him to his recollection untill he threatened to shoot him instantly if he did not take hold of the rudder and do his duty. . . .

The Indian woman, to whom I ascribe equal fortitude and resolution with any person on board at the time of the accident, caught and preserved most of the light articles, which were washed overboard.

MERIWETHER LEWIS

Below: A section of rapids along the Missouri River near Great Falls, Montana.

Thanks to Sacagawea, most of the cargo was saved. After drying out on the riverbank, the items were repacked, and the expedition was on its way once again.

*May 31st 1805. As we passed on it seemed
as if those seens of visionary inchantment
would never have an end.*
MERIWETHER LEWIS

DECISION AT THE MARIAS RIVER

As the expedition passed through unexplored territory, they took careful notes of the geography, plants, and animals. There were no Indians to be seen. They named new rivers they passed after people in the expedition. Soon everybody had a river or creek named after them.

By the end of May, the climate changed. The air was so dry the captains' ink quickly evaporated if not properly covered. There was no morning dew on the grass, and very little rain.

On May 31 the Corps passed through an area now called the White Cliffs of the Missouri. Weathered sandstone formations loomed hundreds of feet above the river.

We passed some very curious cliffs and rocky peaks, in a long range. Some of them 200 feet high and not more than eight feet thick. They seem as if built by the hand of man, and are so numerous that they appear like the ruins of an anctient city.

PATRICK GASS

Left: The White Cliffs area of the Missouri River, east of present-day Fort Benton, Montana. *Far left:* Decision Point, where the Missouri and Marias Rivers meet.

Although the scenery was beautiful, travel became more and more difficult. The cold water was sometimes so shallow the men had to get out and drag the heavy canoes, often over slippery rapids.

On June 2, the Corps camped at a fork in the river. Lewis and Clark couldn't tell which fork was the Missouri. Up to this point, the information they had received from the Hidatsa Indians had been mostly accurate. But they hadn't been told about this river, and now a huge decision had to be made. If they went up the wrong river, they probably couldn't backtrack and make it to the Rocky Mountains in time to cross them before winter set in. In that case, they would probably freeze or starve to death.

Water from the right branch, which veered to the north, was muddy, just as the Missouri River had been all the way from St. Louis. The men were convinced this was the true Missouri. Lewis and Clark thought otherwise. They reasoned that the right branch traveled a long way over the Canadian Plains, which explained its muddy appearance. Water from the left branch was clear, just like a mountain river. The left branch led to the Rocky Mountains, they were certain.

The men were not so sure. But they were a team, and by now almost a family. They were willing to follow their captains anywhere. Lewis wrote in his journal, "They said very cheerfully that they were ready to follow us any where we thought proper to direct, but that they still thought that the other was the [main] river." Lewis named the right branch the Marias River, after a cousin in Virginia.

The men resumed the journey, struggling up the left branch of the river. Lewis pushed on ahead. The Hidatsa Indians had told him they would come upon a mighty waterfall. If he could find the waterfall, it would prove they were on the right track.

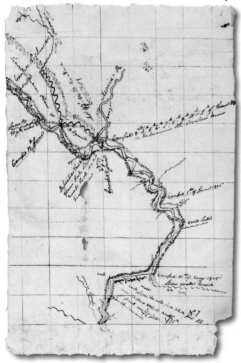

A map drawn by William Clark showing the Marias River emptying into the Missouri River from the north.

A reenactor dressed as Drouillard, one of the expedition's hunters, makes bullets by pouring molten lead, heated by a campfire, into a mold. The expedition had a good supply of lead bars available to make bullets.

To gaze on this sublimely grand specticle. . . .
formes the grandest sight I ever beheld.

MERIWETHER LEWIS
JUNE 13, 1805

THE GREAT FALLS

Captain Lewis, together with four other men, traveled overland ahead of the main expedition. They were trying to find the waterfall the Hidatsa Indians had told them of, which would prove they were on the correct branch of the Missouri River.

On June 13, Lewis heard a faint roaring. In the distance he saw columns of steam rising from the river channel. He hurried on. Seven miles (11 km) later, Lewis walked down a steep ravine and found an incredible spectacle: the Great Falls of the Missouri. The river ran through a narrow gorge cut into the countryside. Roaring like thunder and sending huge columns of spray into the air, the falls were 300 yards (274 m) wide and 80 feet (24 m) high. Lewis had his proof: he and Clark had been right in choosing the left channel as the true Missouri.

Lewis sent a message back to Clark and the rest of the men. He then went on ahead to find the best place to portage, to haul the canoes and equipment around the giant waterfall.

F. J. Haynes took this photo of the Great Falls of the Missouri in 1880. Today, hydroelectric dams reduce the flow over the falls.

As he explored farther upriver, Lewis discovered an unpleasant surprise. After a few miles he encountered another waterfall. Then another. And another. Lewis found five waterfalls in all. To get past them, the expedition had to portage more than 18 miles (29 km) over ravines and broken ground strewn with rocks, rattlesnakes, and prickly pear cactus that pierced the men's moccasins.

The men chopped down the few cottonwoods they could find on the barren landscape. They used the trees to build carts with solid wooden wheels. Leaving the two pirogues behind, they hauled the canoes and cargo around the falls. The going was backbreaking, and slow. Men dislocated their shoulders, were bit by rattlesnakes, or had their feet torn by the rocks and the prickly pears. Plagues of gnats and mosquitoes constantly swarmed around the tormented men.

The beautiful yet painful prickly pear cactus.

At every halt, these poor fellows tumble down and are so much fortiegued that many of them are asleep in an instant;… others faint and unable to stand for a few minutes.

MERIWETHER LEWIS

Lewis & Clark: Adventures West

Sacagawea became very sick. She was so ill Lewis and Clark feared she might die. Not only were they afraid for her and her newborn son, they also needed her to translate with the Shoshone Indians upriver, if they were to have any hope of trading for ponies to get over the mountains. Lewis gave Sacagawea medicine, including water from a nearby sulfur spring he had discovered. Slowly, she recovered.

The portage continued. Days turned into weeks. The intense summer heat was sometimes interrupted by violent thunderstorms. Baseball-sized hail rained down on the unprotected heads of the men, knocking them down and inflicting cuts and bruises. Once, a flash flood nearly swept away Clark, Charbonneau, Sacagawea, and her baby.

Grizzly bears were a constant danger. A hungry bear once caught Lewis alone, his rifle unloaded. Lewis ran as fast as he could, but the bear gained on him by the second. Desperate, Lewis jumped into the river, then wheeled around to face the bear. The grizzly suddenly became frightened and ran off.

William Clark's map of the Great Falls of the Missouri and the portage route taken by the Corps of Discovery.

July 4, 1805. We all believe that we are now about to enter on the most perilous and difficult part of our voyage, yet I see no one repining; all appear ready to meet those difficulties which await us with resolution and becoming fortitude.

MERIWETHER LEWIS

THE THREE FORKS

B y early July, the portage around the Great Falls was finally complete. The men celebrated the Fourth of July with a feast of beans, suet dumplings, and buffalo. That night, Pierre Cruzatte brought out his fiddle, and the men danced and partied until late.

Despite the festive mood, Lewis and Clark were worried. The portage they thought would take half a day had stretched into nearly a month. And looming to the west were the Rocky Mountains, bigger than anything they had ever encountered. Worse, they were still snowcapped, even this late in the season.

The Mountains to the N.W. and West of us are still entierely covered with snow, are white and glitter with the reflection of the sun.

WILLIAM CLARK

Far left: The Three Forks of the Missouri River. *Below:* William Clark's field notes from June 2 to July 10, 1805.

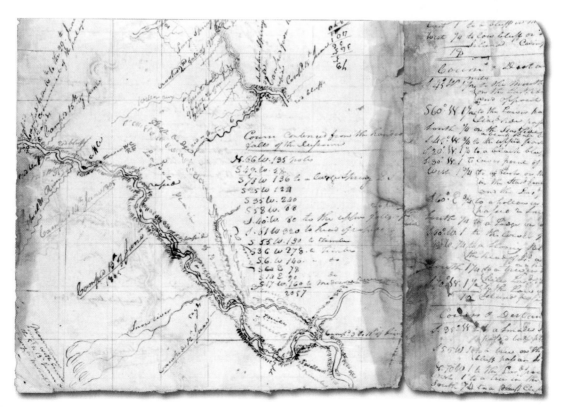

The Gates of the Mountains, near Helena, Montana.

Their next milestone would be the Three Forks of the Missouri, a point where the Missouri splits into three smaller rivers. From there, the Hidatsa Indians had told them, it would be a short journey to the mountains.

As they proceeded on, the Corps found themselves moving south, not west toward the Rockies. The days went by, and still they were no closer to the Continental Divide.

Just north of what is today Helena, Montana, the men passed through a narrow canyon with great cliffs rising up from the water nearly a thousand feet high. Lewis wrote that these were "the most remarkable cliffs that we have yet seen. . . . From the singular appearance of this place, I called it the Gates of the Rocky Mountains."

Lewis & Clark: Adventures West

After passing through the canyon, the men found themselves on a broad plain with "distant and lofty mountains" looming on all sides. Sacagawea recognized the area.

July 22ⁿᵈ. The Indian woman recognizes the country and assures us that this is the river on which her relations live, and that the three forks are at no great distance. this peice of information has cheered the sperits of the party.

MERIWETHER LEWIS

Lewis and Clark at Three Forks, a mural by Edgar S. Paxson, hangs in Montana's state capitol building in Helena.

By the end of July, the Corps finally reached the Three Forks. Lewis and Clark named the three tributaries the Gallatin, after Secretary of the Treasury Albert Gallatin; the Madison, after Secretary of State James Madison; and the Jefferson. Lewis wrote that they called it the Jefferson River "in honor of that illustrious personage Thomas Jefferson, the author of our enterprise."

They camped and rested at the Three Forks for a time, but not for too long. They knew that their next great task would be to find the Shoshone Indians and buy ponies. Without the horses, they would never make it across the mountains.

But there was no sign of the Shoshone, or their horses. The Corps had no choice but to proceed on.

THE JEFFERSON

On August 12, 1805, President Thomas Jefferson received a shipment of materials, which had been sent the previous spring by Lewis and Clark from the Mandan Indian villages in present-day North Dakota. The shipment included samples of Indian corn, elk antlers (which still hang at Jefferson's home at Monticello, Virginia), maps, journals, and two live animals who survived the trip: a magpie and a prairie dog.

After reading Meriwether Lewis's report, Jefferson felt confident. He guessed the Corps of Discovery was already safely camped on the coast of the Pacific Ocean. But in reality, they weren't even close.

July 27, 1805. We begin to feel considerable anxiety with rispect to the Snake [Shoshone] Indians. If we do not find them or some other nation who have horses I fear the successfull issue of our voyage will be very doubtfull.

MERIWETHER LEWIS

By the end of July 1805, the expedition had made it to the Three Forks, the point where three major tributaries of the Missouri River come together. The captains agreed that the right-hand fork, the Jefferson, was the river to follow, since it appeared to lead toward the Rocky Mountains.

Clark estimated they had traveled almost 2,500 miles (4,023 km) from St. Louis. Lewis wrote in his journal that the Three Forks were "an essential point in the geography of this western part of the continent." He took careful readings to mark the point's exact latitude and longitude, and suggested in his notes that the area would make a good location for a fort. The Corps spent two days at the Three Forks, recuperating and repairing their canoes and equipment.

Sacagawea told the captains they were close to the spot where she had been kidnapped five years earlier by a war party of Hidatsa Indians. This lifted the spirits of Lewis and Clark.

The Jefferson River, just above the Three Forks of the Missouri, in southwestern Montana.

Above: Artist John Clymer's *Up the Jefferson* shows William Clark in the lead.

Below right: Wildflowers in bloom along the Jefferson River in Montana.

Sacagawea was a member of the Shoshone nation, which the captains knew kept large herds of ponies. With any luck, they hoped to trade for some of the horses. These would carry the men and supplies over the Continental Divide to the Columbia River system, which led to the Pacific Ocean. But first, they had to locate the Shoshone Indians.

The Jefferson River led west, toward the mountains. It was a clear, swift-flowing stream. The men struggled to pull their dugout canoes up the shallow water. The going was miserable. Gnats and mosquitoes swarmed their faces. They slipped on

A reenactor displays a waterproof lead container used to hold the expedition's gunpowder. When the gunpowder ran out, the containers were melted down to make more bullets.

the rocky riverbed and sprained their ankles and knees. Ropes they used to drag the canoes snapped. Joseph Whitehouse was nearly drowned when a canoe floated over him, trapping him between the streambed and the bottom of the boat.

Prickly pear cacti sliced through the men's moccasins. William Clark's feet became infected, and a large boil on his ankle made him nearly unable to walk. Still, the Corps pressed on toward the mountains.

A replica of Meriwether Lewis's espontoon. In addition to using the steel-pointed staff for self-defense, Lewis also used it to steady his rifle, which helped him to shoot more accurately. In the background is a Native American tepee, similar to the one Lewis and Clark slept in after visiting the Mandan villages of present-day North Dakota. Sacagawea, along with her husband and baby, also slept in the tepee.

August 2nd. The tops of these mountains are yet covered partially with snow, while we in the valley are nearly suffocated with the intense heat of the midday sun; the nights are so cold that two blankets are not more than sufficient covering. . . . Capt. Clark discovers a tumor rising on the inner side of his ankle this evening which was painfull to him.

MERIWETHER LEWIS

The Jefferson forked into smaller streams. Sometimes the Corps took the wrong path, then had to double back several miles. Many of the men wanted to stop dragging the canoes up the river and go instead by foot.

After a week of this torture, there was still no sign of the Shoshones or their horses. The only piece of good news came from Sacagawea, who recognized a rock outcropping called Beaverhead Rock, near present-day Dillon, Montana. They were definitely on the right track.

Beaverhead Rock, near Dillon, Montana.

The Jefferson

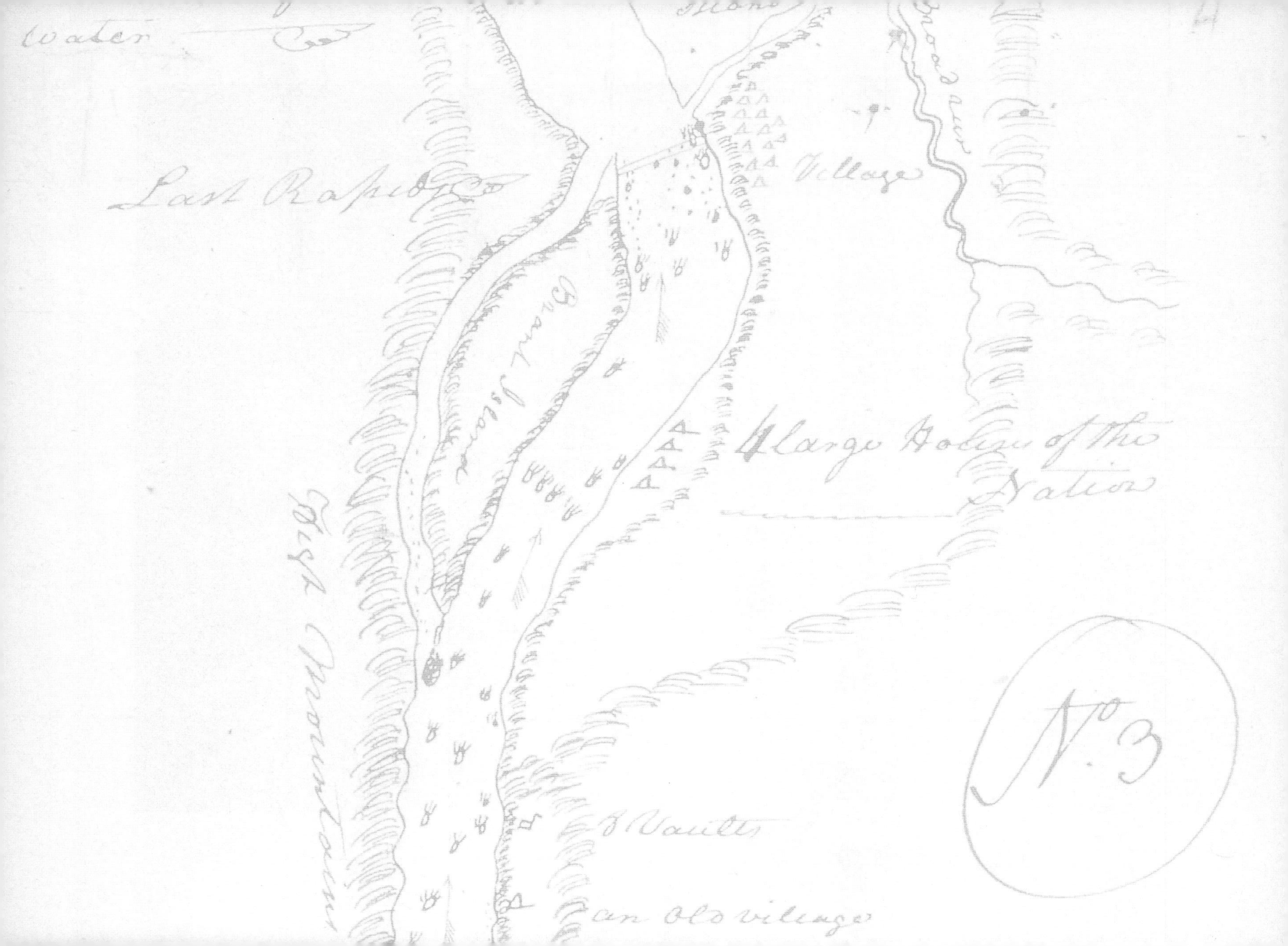

No 3

Broadaur

a Village

a large body of the Nation

Brant Island

High Mountains

Vaults

an old village

Last Rapids

Water

Stone

PART FOUR
THE TERRIBLE MOUNTAINS

August 12th, 1805. At the distance of
4 miles further [up was] the most distant
fountain of the waters of the mighty
Missouri in surch of which we have spent
so many toilsome days and wristless nights.

MERIWETHER LEWIS

THE MOST DISTANT FOUNTAIN

Meriwether Lewis was desperate to contact the Shoshones and secure horses for the mountain trek. On August 9, he and a small group of men set out on foot ahead of the main party. Two days later, they spotted a lone Native American on horseback, the first they had seen since leaving the Mandan villages that spring.

The man stopped some distance away; he seemed suspicious of the strangers. Lewis walked slowly forward, trying to signal that they were friendly. Suddenly, the man turned his horse and vanished into the woods. Perhaps he thought Lewis and his men were Blackfeet or Hidatsa warriors. Whatever the reason, Lewis's hopes were dashed. But still they pressed on.

The next day, August 12, 1805, the same day President Jefferson received his shipment in Washington, D.C., Lewis and his men found a well-worn Indian trail that led west up a gentle slope. A small stream ran down the hill. One of Lewis's men, Hugh McNeal, "stood with a foot on each side of this little rivulet and thanked god that he had lived to bestride the mighty & heretofore deemed endless Missouri." They were at Lemhi Pass, at the western edge of Louisiana Territory.

Right: A black-billed magpie, unknown to science before Lewis & Clark.
Far left: Lemhi Pass, on the border of Montana and Idaho.

August 12, 1805. I discovered immence ranges of high mountains still to the West of us with their tops partially covered with snow.

MERIWETHER LEWIS

Lewis drank from the spring and rested, then continued up the slope. He was bursting with excitement. Just a short walk ahead of him was the ridgeline, and what he believed to be the Continental Divide. On the other side, waters ran west, toward the Pacific Ocean.

If the Rocky Mountains were anything like the Appalachian Mountains back East, Lewis would top the ridge and see sprawled out before him a gentle slope, leading to a plain just like on the eastern side of the mountains. After hundreds of years of searching, the Northwest Passage would at last be found. One of the great prizes of exploration, the main reason Thomas Jefferson had sent the Corps of Discovery out West, would finally be claimed.

Lewis reached the top of the ridge, his heart pounding. He looked west, then froze. In front of Lewis were seemingly endless mountain peaks, as far as the eye could see. Lewis later wrote, "immence ranges of high mountains still to the West of us, with their tops partially covered with snow."

Lewis & Clark: Adventures West

The dream of the Northwest Passage, of an easy water route from coast to coast, died that day. Gone also was Lewis's hope for a quick portage to the Columbia River system. If Lewis was surprised or saddened by the harsh reality of the situation, he never recorded his feelings in his journal. Still, it must have been a shock.

But Lewis was under tremendous pressure, and he didn't have time to reflect. He was separated from Clark and the rest of the expedition, with only three men at his side. A frightened horseman was probably at that moment raising the alarm that strangers were invading Shoshone territory.

Above: A view from Lemhi Pass, looking east toward Montana. *Below:* Spring wildflowers bloom on the trail leading to the Lemhi Pass.

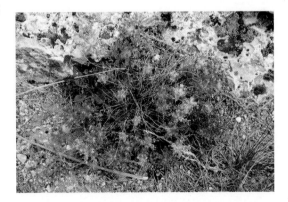

Lewis *had* to make contact with the Native Americans and trade for horses. The very survival of the Corps of Discovery depended on his success, and he was running out of time.

August 13, 1805. We had marched about 2 miles when we met a party of about 60 warriors mounted on excellent horses who came in nearly full speed.

MERIWETHER LEWIS

THE SHOSHONE

After crossing the Continental Divide, Lewis and his men continued westward. They moved down the ridge, which was steeper than the east side. There were gullies and thickets, but the well-worn Indian road was easy to follow. At one point Lewis found "a handsome bold running Creek of cold water. Here I first tasted the water of the great Columbia river."

The group set up camp for a much-needed rest. But by the next day, August 13, they were up early, still following the trail down the long valley.

That morning, Lewis and his men stumbled upon three Shoshone women. One of them, a teenager, fled into the woods, but the other two, an old woman and a young girl of about 12, sat on the ground and held their heads down. They saw no chance to escape from what they thought was an Indian raiding party. Lewis wrote that they seemed ready to die.

Far Left: Newell Convers Wyeth's *Indian War Party.* *Below:* A photo by Andrew Russell of Shoshone warriors on horseback.

Lewis took the old woman by the hand and raised her up. His face, arms, and hands were deeply tanned from months spent in the open sunlight. He rolled his sleeve up to show her that they were white men. He gave them some beads, mirrors, and vermilion to show that the Corps was friendly. The two women were very relieved.

Suddenly, 60 Shoshone warriors came galloping up on horses. They thought they were intercepting a raiding party of Hidatsa Indians. With so many warriors, it would take only a few moments to kill Lewis and his men, if they chose to do so.

Instead of running or defending himself, Lewis ordered his men to stay put. He lowered his rifle to the ground, then followed the old Shoshone woman, who approached the lead rider. Lewis assumed this was the Shoshone chief. Lewis rolled up his sleeve to show his skin. It was the first time the Shoshone had ever seen a white man.

A deer stands in a meadow on the Lemhi Pass. Chief Cameahwait and his people eagerly accepted the gifts of meat offered by Lewis. The Shoshone at that time were on the brink of starvation.

Lewis & Clark: Adventures West

The old woman told the chief that the strangers were friendly. She showed him the presents Lewis had given her. Tensions melted away. The chief got down off his horse and approached Lewis. He put his left arm over Lewis's right shoulder, then pressed his cheek to Lewis's and said "Ah-hi-e." Lewis learned later the words meant "I am much pleased."

The other warriors soon joined in. Wrote Lewis, "We wer all carresed and besmeared with their grease and paint till I was heartily tired of the national hug."

The chief's name was Cameahwait, which means the One Who Never Walks. His village was very poor, having been raided earlier that spring by enemy war parties. Still, they were generous with the newcomers. "They live in a wretched stait of poverty," wrote Lewis, but were "generous with the little they possess," and "extreemly honest."

Montana artist Charles Russell shows Lewis's first meeting with Shoshone chief Cameahwait. To show he was friendly, Lewis dropped his rifle and approached the war party, waving an American flag as a gesture of peace.

Ferns growing along the Lolo Trail in the Bitterroot Mountains.

Through the sign language of George Drouillard, Lewis told Chief Cameahwait that more of his group would soon arrive, and that they needed ponies to travel over the mountains to the west. He invited Cameahwait and his warriors to go back over the Lemhi Pass and meet Clark and the rest of the Corps of Discovery. Many of Cameahwait's people thought it was a trick, that Lewis was luring their chief to an ambush. The lack of an interpreter didn't help matters. To break the language barrier, they would have to negotiate for horses with Charbonneau and Sacagawea present.

Chief Cameahwait agreed to the journey, but he grew wary of the strangers. His suspicions were eased somewhat during the hike across the Lemhi when Lewis's men killed a deer and shared it with the Shoshones. The Indians, who were half starved, gratefully accepted the meat.

On August 17, Lewis linked up with Clark and the rest of the expedition. For the men of the Corps, it was the end of dragging the canoes. They would go overland from here on, until linking up with the Columbia River system somewhere over the Bitterroot Mountains to the west.

But first, they needed ponies. The Shoshone tribe had a herd of over 700, and Lewis was anxious to start negotiations now that he had an interpreter available. Sacagawea was called for. What happened next was one of the great coincidences of all time.

The moccasins of the whole party were taken off, and after much ceremony the smoking began. . . . Glad of an opportunity of being able to converse more intelligibly, Sacagawea was sent for; she came . . . sat down, and was beginning to interpret, when, in the person of Cameahwait, she recognized her brother. She instantly jumped up, and ran and embraced him, throwing over him her blanket, and weeping profusely.

WILLIAM CLARK

Chief Cameahwait was Sacagawea's brother. Any suspicions he had of Lewis and Clark instantly vanished. His long-lost sister had finally returned. Negotiations for the ponies began on a positive note.

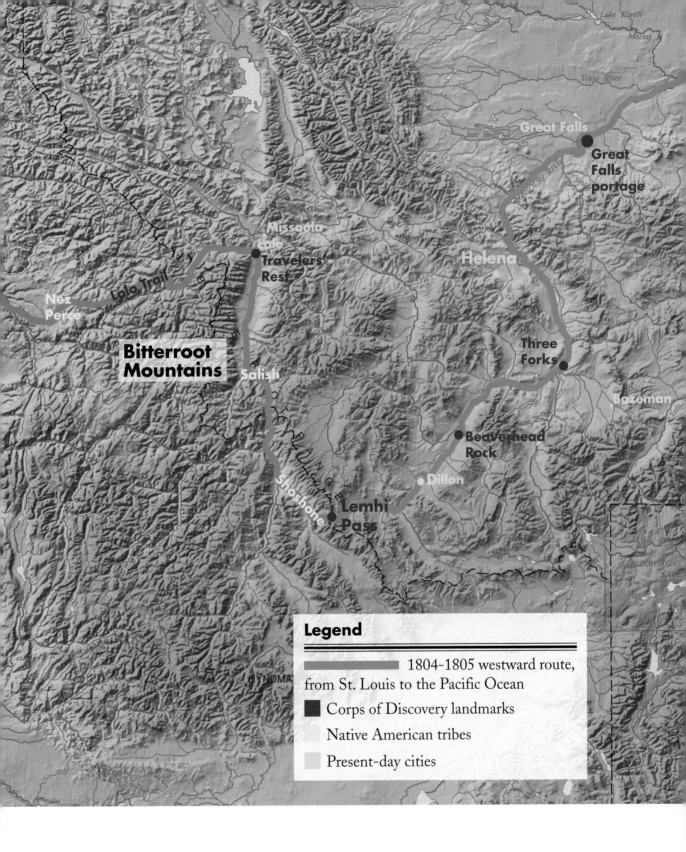

Great Falls

Great
Falls
portage

Missoula
Lolo
Travelers'
Rest

Helena

Lolo Trail

Nez
Percé

Bitterroot
Mountains

Three
Forks

Salish

Bozeman

Beaverhead
Rock

Shoshone

Dillon

Lemhi
Pass

HYNDMA

Legend

1804-1805 westward route,
from St. Louis to the Pacific Ocean

Corps of Discovery landmarks

Native American tribes

Present-day cities

The Shoshone

This is a rock formation along the trail leading to the Continental Divide and Lemhi Pass. Camp Fortunate, just east of this spot, is today covered by the waters of Clark Canyon Reservoir.

Interpreting was a complicated process. The captains made an offer and passed it on to Francois Labiche, who spoke both English and French. Labiche passed the message on to Toussaint Charbonneau, who passed it on to his wife in the Hidatsa language. Sacagawea then translated the Hidatsa into Shoshone for her brother. And then the reply went back in reverse.

Despite the errors in translation that probably occurred, the captains were soon able to buy as many ponies as they needed to cross the Bitterroot Mountains. Cameahwait wanted to start good trade relations with the easterners. If, as Lewis and Clark promised, more traders followed in the years to come, Cameahwait hoped to buy much-needed guns to protect his people from the raiding parties of rival tribes.

Lewis later wrote, "Cameahwait, with his ferce eyes and lank jaws grown meager for the want of food . . . [said,] 'If we had guns, we could live in the country of the buffaloe and eat as our enimies do, and not be compelled to hide ourselves in these mountains and live on roots and berries as the bear do.'"

Lewis & Clark: Adventures West

The deal was settled. For Lewis and Clark, the waiting was over. They finally had their ponies; the trek over the mountains could begin. They were so relieved that they gave their camp a name: Camp Fortunate.

The next day, the men began the long process of portaging their supplies and equipment over the Lemhi Pass to the Shoshone village. It was August 18, Lewis's 31st birthday. He had just become the first American to cross the Continental Divide, and had finally bartered for ponies from the Shoshones so that the expedition could continue. Yet, in his journal entry that day, Lewis seemed depressed. "I had as yet done but little, very little indeed." He vowed "in future, to live for *mankind*, as I have heretofore lived *for myself*."

Perhaps the gloomy journal entry was a sign of Lewis's depression. There had been other hints along the way, such as the long stretches of time when Lewis didn't make any journal entries at all. Lewis probably did suffer from depression, but he seldom let it affect his responsibility to the Corps. It must have taken tremendous willpower to set his feelings aside and continue leading the expedition.

A young Native American woman and her child, photographed by Edward S. Curtis.

September 3rd Tuesday 1805. This day we passed over emence hils and Some of the worst roade that ever horses passed . . . our horses frequently fell . . . Snow about 2 inches deep when it began to rain which termonated in a Sleet[storm].

WILLIAM CLARK

The Most Terrible Mountains

B y early September, the Corps was on the move again. They had spent several days with the Shoshones, studying the people and their culture. But summer was quickly drawing to an end. There were mountains to be crossed.

An old Shoshone man had told Lewis about a trail that was used by the Nez Percé Indians on the western side of the mountains. The Nez Percé used the trail on their way to the Great Plains to hunt buffalo. Lewis and Clark hired the man. Old Toby, as they called him, agreed to guide the Corps to the trail and across the mountains. Sacagawea, for reasons nobody wrote down, continued with the expedition instead of staying with her people. Some believe she had no choice, that she was as much a slave as a wife to Charbonneau.

The Corps traveled north through rugged hills and woods. The Salmon River ran parallel to them, but they couldn't float down it. Clark had scouted ahead and reported that there were too many rapids. It was so dangerous the Indians named it the River of No Return.

Left: John Clymer's painting of the Corps of Discovery struggling through the Bitterroot Mountains.
Right: The River of No Return.

They continued north near the border of today's Montana and Idaho. The going was rough, but they made steady progress, thanks to the 29 horses they bought from the Shoshone Indians. But whenever they looked to their left, the Bitterroot Mountains loomed over them, high and snowcapped. The men knew that soon they would turn west and cross over that seemingly impenetrable mountain barrier, or die trying.

Lewis and Clark Meeting the Flatheads at Ross' Hole, by artist Charles M. Russell. The Salish Indians were called Flatheads by Lewis and Clark. It was a name they used for many Indian tribes of the Northwest. The Salish, however, did not deform their heads like tribes along the Columbia River.

They eventually rode over a mountain pass, then down into the valley of a beautiful river, the Bitterroot. At a place called Ross' Hole, they met a group of about 400 Salish Indians. The tribe had never before seen white men.

The Salish were friends of the Shoshones, and seeing Old Toby helped them accept the strangers. They traded with Lewis and Clark for fresh ponies. The Corps now had 39 horses, three colts, and a mule.

After following the Bitterroot River north for a few more days, the expedition stopped where Lolo Creek empties into the river. Old Toby told them that this was the spot where they would turn west and cross over the mountains. Lewis and Clark decided to camp for two days before trying to climb "those unknown formidable snow clad Mountains." They rested their horses, hunted for food, and took celestial readings for the map of the West that Clark was making for President Jefferson. Lewis called their camp Travelers' Rest.

On September 11, the Corps started climbing up the Bitterroot Mountains, which Sergeant Patrick Gass called "the most terrible mountains I ever beheld."

They followed the Nez Percé path, which today is called the Lolo Trail. Even today the area is one of the most remote and wild places in the country. When the expedition went through the area, there was very little game to hunt—most animals lived down on the fertile Plains. (Today, big-game animals have been driven up into the mountains by human development.) The expedition soon ran short of food. The horses were starving from a lack of grass to eat.

The trail was miserable. Fallen timber blocked the way. The ground was steep and slippery, especially when it rained. On September 14, the weather got worse and worse: rain and hail turned to sleet, then snow. Freezing wind cut through the men's clothing. Clark wrote, "I have been wet and as cold in every part as I ever was in my life."

The Bitterroot Mountains almost cost the members of the Corps their lives. Lewis and Clark saw this section of the mountains to their left as they travelled north toward camp at Travelers' Rest, near present-day Missoula, Montana.

Above: Nootka Rose, growing alongside the Lolo Trail.

Far right: The Lolo Trail exists today much as it did when Lewis and Clark passed through. It was an old trail used extensively by the Nez Percé, who lived west of the Bitterroot Range.

Old Toby lost the trail in the snow. Instead of following the ridgeline, he wandered down into a streambed tangled with dense brush. He eventually realized his mistake, then led the expedition back up the mountainside, "as steep as the roof of a house." They lost two days because of the mistake. Still the weather worsened. Still there was nothing to eat.

To keep from starving to death they were forced to butcher one of the colts. They melted snow for drinking water. They called the stream near their camp Colt Killed Creek.

After five days of struggling over the trail, Clark climbed up a ridge and looked west. His heart sank. "From this mountain, I could observe high rugged mountains in every direction, as far as I could see."

Some of the horses, weak from exhaustion and a lack of food, slipped off the trail. Once Lewis's horse lost its footing and fell, nearly crushing the captain to death.

September 16. When we awoke this morning, to our great surprise, we were covered with snow, which had fallen about 2 inches the later part of last night, and it continues a very cold snowstorm. . . . Some of the men without socks, wrapped rags on their feet, and we loaded up our horses and set out without anything to eat, and proceeded on. We could hardly see the old trail for the snow.

JOSEPH WHITEHOUSE

We came to the highest part of the mountain, we halted. . . . The Mountains continue as far as our eyes could extend. They extend much further than we expected.

JOHN ORDWAY

Lewis & Clark: Adventures West

One of many mountain streams that empty into the Lochsa River in the Bitterroot Mountains. The Lochsa runs roughly parallel to the Lolo Trail.

It was too late to turn back. In desperation, Clark and six others went ahead, trying to find food and a way out of the mountains.

The food situation grew critical. Another colt was butchered. They ate an occasional grouse, a coyote, or crayfish caught in the mountain streams. Mostly they went hungry. The men suffered from the first stages of malnutrition: weakness, skin rashes, diarrhea. Lewis knew the expedition was on the verge of destruction. "I find myself growing weak for the want of food," he wrote, "and most of the men complain of a similar deficiency and have fallen off very much."

Frozen and nearly starved to death, the Corps of Discovery, including Sacagawea and her infant son, was forced to march onward or die in the mountains. But they were tough and disciplined, and trusted their leaders.

Finally, on September 21, they came upon a small open bottom area where there was enough grass for the horses to eat. The next day, Lewis led his men out of the mountains and into a fertile valley.

Lewis & Clark: Adventures West

The ordeal lasted 11 torturous days, covering 160 miles (257 km) from Travelers' Rest. They wandered out of the Bitterroot wilderness half-dead, more weak and vulnerable than they had ever been. But they were victorious over the mountains, thanks to their discipline, the leadership of Lewis and Clark, and the guidance of Old Toby.

But as soon as they emerged from the Bitterroots, the expedition faced another danger: the mighty Nez Percé tribe, the most powerful in the region.

As the members of the Corps staggered into a Nez Percé village, looking for food and drink, the Native Americans gathered to debate. What would they do with these strangers, these weak and hungry white men who were rich with tools and guns? Befriend them—or kill them?

Wildflowers from the Bitterroot Mountains.

Famed frontier photographer Edward S. Curtis took this image of a Nez Percé warrior at the turn of the 20th century.

CLARK 19th Novr 1805

Chinnook River

PART FIVE
TO THE PACIFIC

*September 22nd 1805. The pleasure I now
felt in having tryumphed over the rocky
Mountains . . . can be more readily
conceived than expressed.*

MERIWETHER LEWIS

THE REAL PEOPLE

In the autumn of 1805, Meriwether Lewis led the Corps of Discovery out of the Bitterroot Mountains. After 11 exhausting days, with little or nothing to eat, they staggered out of the the wilderness frail and open to attack—right in the middle of the most powerful Native American tribe in the Pacific Northwest.

Several days earlier, Captain William Clark and six other men had gone ahead in a desperate attempt to find food. They found a horse, which they killed and butchered. Along with the horsemeat, Clark left a note for Captain Lewis, telling him that he intended to push onward as quickly as possible. He hoped to make it off the mountains and onto the plains, where game was more plentiful.

When the main expedition found the horse Clark had left for them, Captain Lewis was optimistic that their ordeal through the mountains was nearing an end. Finding the horse

meant that Native Americans were nearby. In his journal, Lewis wrote that they "made a hearty meal on our horse beef much to the comfort of our hungry stomachs."

Left: Black Eagle, a Nez Percé warrior, photographed by Edward S. Curtis a century after Lewis and Clark.
Far left: A grove of cedar trees growing along the Lolo Trail in the Bitterroot Mountains, in present-day Idaho.

On September 22, 1805, they emerged from the mountains. Somehow, they had avoided freezing to death, or falling to their doom over the narrow mountain pathway. They were half starved, but they were in open country now. By the end of the day, they came to an Indian village of 18 lodges near present-day Weippe, Idaho. The Native Americans welcomed the Corps of Discovery. They called themselves Nimiipu—"the real people."

William Clark, who arrived at the village days earlier, had already started taking notes on the tribe's sophisticated, complex society. They were skilled warriors, but they also prized family relationships. The elderly were honored most of all.

A Nez Percé warrior chief, photographed by Edward S. Curtis.

Through the sign language of one of the French-Canadian interpreters, Clark made a faulty translation of their name, calling them "pierced nose," or Nez Percé, even though nose piercing wasn't a common practice among the tribe.

Lewis & Clark: Adventures West

Clark befriended one of the chiefs, an older man called Twisted Hair. On a white elkskin, Twisted Hair drew a map of the area west of the villages. Clark learned that the nearby Clearwater River joined with the Snake River, which in turn emptied into the Columbia River. The Corps' days of trekking overland were over. Soon they would be back on the water, paddling downstream this time, speeding toward the Pacific Ocean.

A table filled with tools similar to the kind used on the Lewis & Clark expedition.

Clark joined Lewis and the main party on the night of September 22. Clark wrote in his journal, "I found Capt Lewis & the party Encamped, much fatigued, & hungery, much rejoiced to find something to eate of which They appeared to partake plentifully."

Through his own bad experience, Clark warned them not to overeat the dried salmon and camas roots given by the Nez Percé. In his journal entry two days earlier, he had written, "I find myself verry unwell all the evening from eateing the fish & roots too freely." The next day he wrote, "I am verry Sick today and puke."

The Clearwater River, which Lewis and Clark paddled down toward the Columbia River.

The men didn't heed Clark's warning—they were starving and needed to eat. They gorged themselves on the food the Nez Percé provided. Soon they too became violently ill, suffering severe diarrhea and vomiting. They had lived on a diet of meat for so long that the switch to fish and roots probably caused terrible indigestion. There also may have been bacteria on the fish, which further sickened the men.

To make matters worse, Clark gave the men several doses of "Rush's Thunderbolts," medicine they had brought with them from the East. Lewis and Clark believed the pills could cure almost any illness with their powerful laxative effect. But it was exactly the wrong treatment for the ailing men. The diarrhea got more severe and caused dehydration, which only made them sicker.

Over the next two weeks, the men suffered. Lewis was especially ill. Clark wrote, "Capt Lewis Scercely able to ride on a jentle horse. . . . Several men So unwell that they were Compelled to lie on the Side of the [trail]."

While the Corps was incapacitated by illness, the Nez Percé met secretly to decide what to do with these weak strangers who were so wealthy with weapons and tools. The men of the expedition were the first white people the Nez Percé had ever encountered. There was serious talk of killing them and taking their possessions, which would be an easy enough task. The Corps' modern rifles would make the Nez Percé extremely powerful.

An old woman stepped forward, begging her people to spare the strangers' lives. Her name was Watkuweis, which meant Returned from a Faraway Country. As a young girl, she had been kidnapped by Blackfeet Indians, then sold into slavery. While in Canada, she was befriended by white people. She finally escaped and somehow found her way back to the Nez Percé villages.

A Nez Percé named Many Moons told how Watkuweis shared her story with the tribe: "She told history about the whites and every Nez Percé listened . . . told how the white people were good to her, treated her with kindness. That is why the Nez Percé never made harm to the Lewis and Clark people. . . . We ought to have a monument to her in this far West. She saved much for the white race."

Once again, an Indian woman saved the Corps. First an old Shoshone woman, then Sacagawea, and now Watkuweis. Lewis and Clark owed much of their success to Native Americans, which they barely acknowledged in their journals. Seventy-two years later, in 1877, the U.S. Army drove Chief Joseph and the Nez Percé from Idaho. Among Chief Joseph's people were old men and women who were children when Lewis and Clark passed through, and who remembered the kindness and restraint Twisted Hair's people had shown the Corps of Discovery.

Raven Blanket, a Nez Percé chief photographed by Edward S. Curtis.

October 8th 1805. Set out at 9 oClock passed 15 rapids . . . one canoe in which Serjt. Gass was Stearing and was nearle turning over, She Sprung a leak or split open on one Side and Bottom filled with water & Sunk on the rapid.

WILLIAM CLARK

DOWNSTREAM

Rapids of the Clearwater River.

or nearly two weeks the Corps of Discovery worked at building five dugout canoes, in between bouts of diarrhea and vomiting. They worked in a grove of ponderosa pine trees along the Clearwater River. They called the place Canoe Camp. They chopped down several trees, but they were too weak to use their tools to hollow out the boats. Chief Twisted Hair showed them an easier Indian method that used a slow-burning fire trench to burn out the logs.

The men were feeling better from their sickness, but the recovery was slow.

October 5th. Capt Lewis & my Self eate a Supper of roots boiled, which filled us So full of wind, that we were Scercely able to Breathe all night.

WILLIAM CLARK

Twisted Hair promised to care for the Corps' 38 remaining ponies until they returned the next spring. Lewis had each horse marked by cutting its forelock, the top part of its mane. Twisted Hair also agreed to go partway downstream with the Corps, guiding them and informing other Native Americans that they came in peace. Another chief, Tetoharsky, also joined them.

On October 7, they pushed their five dugout canoes into the Clearwater River. Finally, they had a swift current behind them. Spirits soared, even though many of the men were still weak and sick. Twisted Hair told them it would be a journey of only a couple of weeks until they reached the ocean.

The expedition raced down the Clearwater, then linked up with the Snake River. They encountered many bad rapids along the way. Still, they preferred running the rapids to the time-consuming process of portaging their canoes and baggage. The season was getting on, and Lewis and Clark knew they had to set up a fort on the coast before winter set in. Also, a growing sense of triumph infected the men. They were close, very close indeed, to their goal of crossing the continent. They were in a hurry; the rapids slowed them down, but they still managed to travel up to 30 miles (48 km) a day.

Gradually the men recovered, gaining strength day by day. They grew more daring in shooting the roaring whitewater, despite the cumbersome design of the dugout canoes. It was dangerous work: the canoes were tossed about and swamped, or crashed on rocks and sprang leaks. Old Toby, the Shoshone Indian who had safely guided the Corps over the Bitterroot Mountains, was so scared of the rapids that one morning he took off for home, leaving without pay.

John Clymer's *Angry River* shows the Corps shooting the rapids of the Columbia River system.

A sketch of a white salmon trout from the Lewis and Clark journals.

Native Americans were everywhere. They gathered on the riverbanks and watched as the canoes passed by. They arrived in camp at night to trade, swap stories, or be entertained by Pierre Cruzatte's fiddle playing and the men's dancing.

When they were on the Great Plains, the expedition often went hundreds of miles in between Indian settlements. Here, they saw Native Americans almost every day. Nez Percé, Wananpum, Yakima, and Walla Walla Indians turned out by the hundreds to see the strangers. Luckily, most were friendly. Twisted Hair and Tetoharsky went ahead and informed their relatives that the white men were coming. The presence of Sacagawea also helped. She was a sign to the Indians that the white people came in peace.

The sight of this Indian woman, wife to one of our interprs. confirmed those people of our friendly intentions, as no woman ever accompanies a war party of Indians in this quarter.

WILLIAM CLARK

A Wishram fisherman nets salmon in the Columbia River.

Soon the expedition made it to the Columbia River. They were astonished at the millions of salmon swimming in the crystal-clear waters. The Walla Walla tribe, which lived on the banks of the Columbia, depended on salmon, and had plenty to trade. But the men of the Corps didn't want to risk getting sick again. They wanted meat. They traded with the Walla Wallas for dozens of dogs, which they eagerly ate. Everyone, that is, except William Clark. "Our diet extremely bad," he wrote.

They were moving through a semi-desert now. Game was scarce, and so was firewood. Instead of sending out teams of hunters, they saved time by purchasing dogs from the Indians. Lewis said the diet of dog meat kept the men healthy, but Clark hated it. "As for my own part," he wrote in his journal, "I have not become reconsiled to the taste of this animal."

A journal page showing the intersection of the Snake, Columbia, and Yakima Rivers.

October 24, 1805. We passed safe, to the astonishment of all the Indians.

WILLIAM CLARK

WATERFALLS

On October 19, 1805, Captain Clark climbed a tall cliff and saw, off in the distance, a snow-covered mountain he thought was Mount St. Helens. Even though it was actually Mount Adams, Clark had spied the Cascade Range, which had been seen 13 years earlier by British explorers coming up the Columbia from the Pacific side. Lewis and Clark were back on the map. They had crossed a continent and connected east with west.

On October 23, they entered a 55-mile (89-km) stretch of the river with narrow channels surrounded by towering cliffs. The Columbia River Gorge contained a series of spectacular and dangerous waterfalls and rapids. The first was Celilo Falls. They were forced to portage around most of it. They lowered their canoes down part of it with sections of rope made from elkskin. Local Indians helped carry the baggage around the falls.

The Indians in the area were Chinooks, enemies of the Nez Percé. At a place called The Dalles, Twisted Hair and Tetoharsky said goodbye to Lewis and Clark and began the long journey home.

Far left: A waterfall tumbles toward the mighty Columbia River Gorge.
Below: Celilo Falls, photographed by Benjamin Gifford in 1900. The falls no longer exist today. They were submerged when a hydroelectric dam was built in 1957.

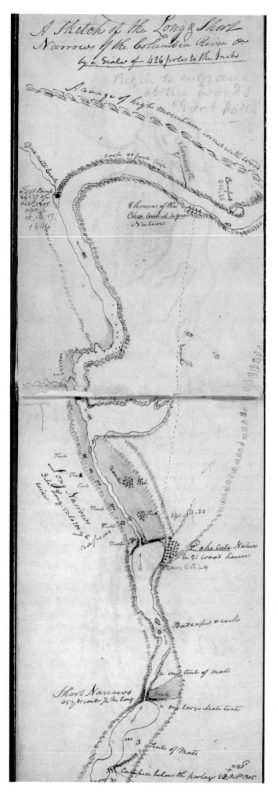

At a raging waterfall called the Short Narrows of The Dalles, Clark and Cruzatte, the Corps' best boatman, went to a high cliff to scout the river. The Chinook Indians said the whitewater was impassable. Clark and Cruzatte thought otherwise, even though Clark was aghast at "the horrid appearance of this agitated gut Swelling, boiling & whorling in every direction."

Clark had the men portage the most important cargo around the falls, including the journals, the rifles and ammunition, plus the scientific instruments. Today the Short Narrows would be classified a Class V rapid, too dangerous to run even with the best equipment. Clark and Cruzatte pushed off into the swirling current with a cumbersome dugout canoe.

Hundreds of Indians watched from the cliffs above, waiting to see the crazy white men kill themselves in the furious current. They were also eager to help themselves to any cargo that might wash up after the strangers had drowned. But Clark and Cruzatte shot straight through. "We passed safe," Clark wrote, "to the astonishment of all the Indians." Clark was pleased with himself, although, he wrote, "from the top of the rock [the water] did not appear as bad as when I was in it."

A sketch of the Long and Short Narrows of the Columbia River, from the journals of Lewis and Clark.

The Corps ran other "impassable" rapids going through the Columbia River Gorge, although sometimes they were forced to portage. Finally, on November 2, they made it past the final waterfall. On November 3 they passed and named Beacon Rock. At this point they began noticing the Columbia River rising and falling with the tide. The ocean couldn't be far away.

Beacon Rock, in present-day Washington, along the north shore of the Columbia River.

November 7th 1805. A cloudy foggey morning, a little rain. Set out at 8 oClock. Proceeded on.

WILLIAM CLARK

TO THE OCEAN

After passing through the raging falls of the Columbia River Gorge, the expedition entered a new climate zone. It was wet most of the time, because the winds from the ocean stalled against the Cascade Range and produced a steady drizzle. Lush forests filled with fir, ash, and spruce enveloped both shores. The trees were huge, the biggest the men had ever seen. Waterfalls poured down from the surrounding cliffs. Dense fog blanketed the river valley. Sometimes the morning fog was so thick they had to wait for hours before setting out.

The river hosted a multitude of geese, swans, ducks, and brants. A happy William Clark was finally able to eat roast duck, setting aside the dog meat that caused him so much distress.

The expedition passed many Chinook Indian villages. The Native Americans often visited the Corps when they were camped for the night. Lewis and Clark thought the Chinooks were highly skilled at making canoes and navigating them in rough water. But for the most part the captains didn't much like the Chinooks. There were several reasons for this, including a language barrier. The Corps had no interpreters that spoke Chinookan, and the Chinooks didn't use sign language like the Nez Percé or the Plains Indian tribes. Lewis and Clark used Chinook Jargon, which was a very basic language combining Chinook, English, French, and Nootka. Translations were often garbled, and misunderstandings caused bad feelings.

The Columbia River widened as the Corps paddled closer to the ocean.

The Chinook tribes were used to trading with European ships that passed by the mouth of the Columbia River. These Europeans often dealt in the sea otter trade. The Chonooks knew how to drive a hard bargain, and Lewis and Clark grew to resent the high prices they were forced to pay for food.

More seriously, some of the Chinooks engaged in petty theft when visiting camp. As the expedition's supply of trade goods dwindled, the captains grew more and more angry.

Adding to their discomfort was the constant rain. Everything became waterlogged. "We are all wet cold and disagreeable," wrote Clark in his journal. Still they paddled downstream, the river widening as they went.

Finally, on the afternoon of November 7, a fog lifted off the river, revealing a most welcome sight. The men shouted as William Clark reached for his notebook and jotted down his now-famous words: "Ocian in view! O! the joy."

That night in camp, he wrote in his journal, "Great joy in camp we are in view of the Ocian, this great Pacific Octean which we have been So long anxious to See. And the roreing or

noise made by the waves braking on the rockey Shores may be heard distinctly."

Clark calculated the distance they had traveled since leaving St. Louis and came up with a staggering 4,142 miles (6,666 km). His estimate would later be proven accurate to within 40 miles (64 km), a remarkable feat of dead reckoning.

Dense, moss-laden forests line the Columbia River Estuary.

William Clark's famous journal entry of November 7, 1805: "Ocian in view! O! the joy."

*November 18, 1805. Men appear much
Satisfied with their trip beholding with
estonishment the high waves dashing against
the rocks & this emence ocian.*

WILLIAM CLARK

CAPE DISAPPOINTMENT

*W*hat Clark thought was the Pacific was actually an estuary of the ocean, the eastern end of Gray's Bay. The ocean was still 20 miles (32 km) away. As the expedition paddled toward the mouth of the Columbia River, fierce winter weather settled in, sending high waves crashing down on their dugout canoes. They were forced to retreat to shore.

For nearly three weeks they were pinned down on the north side of the river. With high cliffs at their backs and raging water in front of them, they were often trapped. They made a series of stops, clawing their way downstream and camping in small, virtually unprotected coves, as giant waves lashed against the shore. Thunder, lightning, and high winds added to the misery. Huge driftwood logs, many feet thick and some over 200 feet (61 m) long, crashed into camp as the swells surged upward. Clark wrote that it was "the most disagreeable time I have experienced."

On November 15 they camped on a sandy beach. The waves were too high for them to pass any farther. It was the end of the trail west for the expedition.

Far left: Flowers growing on a cliff overlooking the Pacific Ocean. *Below:* A storm lashes Oregon's Cannon Beach, south of the mouth of the Columbia River.

Beach grasses flutter in the wind near present-day Seaside, Oregon.

They set up camp, and then for several days Lewis and Clark did some exploring of the north shore. Most of the men stayed in camp, warmed by their fires and marveling at their accomplishment. "Men appear much Satisfied with their trip," wrote Clark, "beholding with estonishment the high waves dashing against the rocks & this emence ocian."

The small expeditions exploring the north shore were looking for food, and for European trading vessels. If they were lucky, they could flag one down and trade for supplies, or even a ride back to the East. But they had no such luck.

Our officers named this Cape, Cape disappointment, on account of not finding Vessells there.

JOSEPH WHITEHOUSE

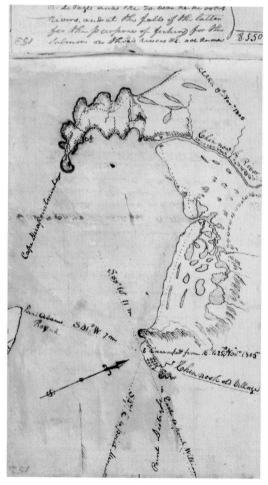
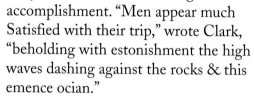

William Clark's map of the mouth of the Columbia River. Although Joseph Whitehouse thought Lewis and Clark named Cape Disappointment, it actually got its name years earlier by a seafaring explorer who had trouble navigating into the river.

On November 24, everyone was called together. A decision had to be made: where would they spend the winter? They could stay on the north side of the Columbia, but there wasn't much game, and the Chinook Indians were charging high prices for food. They could paddle across the estuary to the south side, in present-day Oregon, where there were more elk and where the Clatsop Indians seemed more willing to trade at reasonable prices. Or they could move back upstream where it was drier, perhaps to the Nez Percé villages.

They captains called for a vote. It was an extraordinary moment. They could have simply made a decision and forced the others to obey; it was a military expedition, after all. But they had grown to be a family, a group of people who worked as a team, and every team-member's voice counted. York, Clark's slave, was allowed to vote, almost 60 years before slaves were freed in the United States. Sacagawea also voted, more than 100 years before women or Indians became full citizens.

Sea gulls scavenge for food along a beach in Oregon. In the background is Tillamook Head.

Cape Disappointment

141

23rd March 1806. At this place we had wintered and remained from the 7th of Decr. 1805 to this day and have lived as well as we had any right to expect.

William Clark

FORT CLATSOP

*T*he majority of the party voted to cross the Columbia and spend the winter on the south side of the river. It would still be wet and stormy, but there were more elk to hunt. Plus, there was a chance they might spot a passing ship and hitch a ride home. And even if a ship never came, there was no rush to press eastward: they had to wait until July at the earliest for the snows to melt before they could cross the Bitterroot Mountains.

After a treacherous crossing of the storm-tossed estuary, the Corps set up camp a few miles from the coast. They found a good freshwater supply in a spruce forest on a river near present-day Astoria, Oregon. There they built Fort Clatsop, which they named after the friendly Clatsop Indian tribe.

By Christmas of 1805, they moved into their new fort. It was a log stockade 50 feet (15 m) square. Two rows of cabins were separated by a small parade ground. On one side were the enlisted men's quarters, plus storage rooms. On the other side were the captains' quarters, a meat storage room, and a room for Toussaint Charbonneau, Sacagawea, and their infant son, Jean Baptiste.

During the winter, Lewis and Clark worked on their maps and journals, generally noting everything that had happened to them on the journey so far.

Right: A reenactor at Fort Clatsop National Memorial demonstrates how the men fired their rifles.
Left: The reconstruction of Fort Clatsop was built near the original site in 1955, southwest of Astoria, Oregon.

In January 1806, a whale washed ashore on Cannon Beach, south of the Corps' salt-making camp. They bought 300 pounds (136 kg) of blubber from the Tillamook Indians to supplement their meager diet at Fort Clatsop.

January 17th. Continued stormey all last night, and this morning Wet & rainey.

JOSEPH WHITEHOUSE

The men, meanwhile, kept busy hunting elk and deer, making candles and moccasins, sewing clothes, and boiling sea water to make salt. They were preparing for the long journey home in the spring, and they were anxious to get going. The men were homesick, and the dreary weather didn't help. It rained on all but 12 days during their stay at Fort Clatsop. The food was bad: in the wet weather, meat spoiled very quickly. To make matters worse, the men were infested with fleas, which, Clark wrote, "torment us in such a manner as to deprive us of half the nights Sleep."

Ferns and moss grow on the damp roof of Lewis and Clark's quarters at Fort Clatsop. For most of their stay at the fort, the weather was "rainy, wet, and disagreeable."

Lewis & Clark: Adventures West

There were frequent visits by Clatsop and Chinook Indians, but the Corps was quickly running out of gifts to use as trade barter. Everything was in short supply, and they still had half a continent to cross. They would be heading home this time, however, and once they crossed the Bitterroot Mountains, the Missouri River would propel them downstream all the way to St. Louis.

But before they reached civilization, before they could be reunited with their families, they first had to wait out the winter in the dreary, boring, wet confines of Fort Clatsop.

Then they could go home.

Above: John Clymer's *Sacagawea at the Big Water.*
Below left: A reproduction of the salt camp the Corps ran near present-day Seaside, Oregon, about 10 miles (16 km) from Fort Clatsop. Seawater was boiled in five buckets placed on top of fire-heated rocks. After the water evaporated, salt was scraped off the insides of the buckets.

Camp
22. & 23.
oct. 1805.

Portage 120 yards

Fish
Stacks

rock

feet In:
37-8
feet fall

Great whirl of
about 3 feet

PART SIX
THE JOURNEY HOME

March 23, 1806. We loaded our Canoes
& at 1 P.M. left Fort Clatsop on our
homeward bound journey.

WILLIAM CLARK

HOMEWARD BOUND

In January 1806, a group of 45 Native Americans from 11 different tribes visited President Thomas Jefferson in Washington, D.C. The president welcomed the delegation of Missouri, Oto, Arikara, and Yankton Sioux chiefs, and arranged for a tour of the city so they could witness the power of the United States. They talked about trade, and how the Indians could benefit from American companies setting up outposts in Louisiana Territory. Jefferson stressed how important it was that the tribes be at peace with one another so that the United States and the Native American tribes "may all live together as one household."

The chiefs were impressed with U.S. technology and the country's huge cities. They also spoke highly of Lewis and Clark, who had visited the tribes on their way west the previous year. It was through Lewis and Clark's invitation that the Indians were visiting Washington, D.C. President Jefferson referred to Lewis as "our beloved man," and thanked the Native American chiefs for the kindness they had shown the Corps of Discovery.

Charles Bird King painted this portrait of Omaha, Kansas, Missouri, and Pawnee Indians during their visit to the East in 1821. The man in front is wearing a Jefferson peace medal.

The chiefs responded, "We have seen the beloved man, we shook hands with him and we heard the words you put in his mouth. We wish him well. . . . We have him in our hearts, and when he will return we believe that he will take care of us, prevent our wants and make us happy."

Despite their friendship with Lewis and Clark, the chiefs were troubled. White settlers were starting to take over Native American lands. The delegation gave this warning to Jefferson: "When you tell us that your children of this side of the Mississippi hear your word, you are mistaken, since every day they raise their tomahawks over our heads. . . . Tell your white children on our lands to follow your orders and to do not as they please, for they do not keep your word."

President Jefferson assured the chiefs that he would do all he could to make sure settlers obeyed the treaties with the Native Americans. But in reality, there wasn't much Jefferson could do. On the vast, lawless frontier, trappers and prospectors were starting what would become a tidal wave of settlements, and there was no way to stop them. It was the beginning of the end for the Indian nations.

Jefferson wrote a note to Lewis's mother and brother. He told them he was confident that Lewis was alive and well. But privately, in a letter to naturalist William Dunbar, Jefferson wrote, "We have no certain information of Capt. Lewis since he left Fort Mandan." A year had passed since the Corps had left the Mandan villages in present-day North Dakota. Nobody knew for sure what had become of the explorers. All Jefferson could do was wait, and hope.

Not any occurences today worthy of notice.

WILLIAM CLARK

As President Jefferson met with the Native American chiefs, Meriwether Lewis, William Clark, and the Corps of Discovery were stuck in Fort Clatsop, enduring a typical stormy Oregon winter. The fort was a cramped, wooden stockade. Routine at the camp was unbearably dull. The men's spirits were further sapped by the dampness brought on by almost continual bad weather.

Everybody was homesick. The food was bad, and everything was soggy. Most of the men suffered from colds or flu. The local Clatsop and Chinook Indians, who were used to the climate, were doing well, but they demanded steep payment for food and supplies. The Corps' barter goods were nearly gone. The only thing they had plenty of were rifles and lead, and pens and ink for the journals.

After five long months on the Pacific coast, they hadn't spotted a single ship. They had hoped to hitch a ride home, or at least send copies of their precious journals back to President Jefferson by sea, but it was not to be.

The men had pent-up energy and were ready to go home. On March 23, 1806, they set their canoes in the water and began the long journey home. Before they left, they stole a badly needed canoe from the Clatsop Indians.

Throughout the trip Lewis and Clark had been respectful of the Native Americans they met. The Indians remembered Lewis and Clark for their honesty and friendliness. Yet Lewis ordered his men to steal a canoe. Maybe he felt he had no choice. He badly needed another boat, but couldn't afford the high prices the Clatsops were charging. In his journal, Lewis justified the theft by saying it was in exchange for six elk the Clatsops stole from the Corps. He failed to mention, however, that the Indians later paid for the elk.

Without the Clatsops' help, the Corps might not have survived that winter. The stolen canoe was a friendship betrayed, a lapse of judgement that tarnished the Corps' reputation.

Edward S. Curtis took this photograph of a canoe built by Indians of the Pacific Northwest.

June 14, 1806. Even now I Shudder with the expectation with great dificuelties in passing those Mountains, from the debth of Snow and the want of grass Sufficient [for] . . . our horses.

WILLIAM CLARK

BACK TO THE MOUNTAINS

Paddling upstream against the current of the Columbia River was hard work, and the going was slow. The spring salmon run had not yet begun, and food was scarce. Indians along the riverbanks that the Corps met charged high prices for roots and fish.

The expedition had to portage its heavy canoes over the many falls and rapids of the Columbia. As they hauled their gear along the shore, Indians constantly followed the men, harassing them and stealing small items like axes or tomahawks.

One day a group of Indians stole Lewis's big Newfoundland dog, Seaman. Lewis was so enraged he ordered his men to march into a village and burn it down unless his dog was returned. Luckily for all involved, the thieves gave back the dog after a brief chase.

A pair of elk graze in a mountain meadow. After months of living on nothing but elk, roots, and fish, the men of the Corps were anxious to get back to the Great Plains, where buffalo were plentiful.

Lewis drew this small eulachon, also called a candlefish, in his journal while at Fort Clatsop. He wrote, "I think them superior to any fish I ever tasted."

April 11th. Many of the natives crouded about the bank of the river where the men were engaged in taking up the canoes; one of them had the insollence to cast stones down . . . at the men. . . . These are the greatest thieves and scoundrels we have met with.

MERIWETHER LEWIS

Lewis had developed a very short temper. Once, when a saddle and robe were stolen, he again threatened to burn down a village. Violence was averted when the items were eventually found. Some historians think Lewis was suffering from depression, which ran in his family. Or it could be that he was worried for the safety of his men. They had endured so much, traveled so far, and discovered so many things. But it would all be for nothing if they couldn't get themselves, and the precious journals and scientific specimens, back to civilization.

There were many obstacles yet to come, not the least of which were the Bitterroots, the same terrible mountains that had nearly killed them the previous autumn. In his journal, Lewis tried to steady his nerves by reminding himself, "Patience, patience."

At Celilo Falls, the expedition abandoned the river. They bought 13 ponies at very high prices from a local Indian tribe. Traveling overland was faster than paddling against the swift river current, but the journey was still difficult. They didn't have much success hunting for food. Instead, they bought dogs to eat from the Indians, just as they had done on the westward journey. To help pay for the dogs, Clark exchanged medical services, which the Indians gladly accepted.

When they reached the territory of the Walla Walla tribe, their chief, Yellept, greeted the expedition warmly. They stayed three days, partying and exchanging gifts. Their relationship was much friendlier than with the Indians they encountered on the lower part of the Columbia. Of the Walla Wallas, Lewis wrote, "I think we can justly affirm to the honor of these people that they are the most hospitable, honest, and sincere people that we have met with in our voyage."

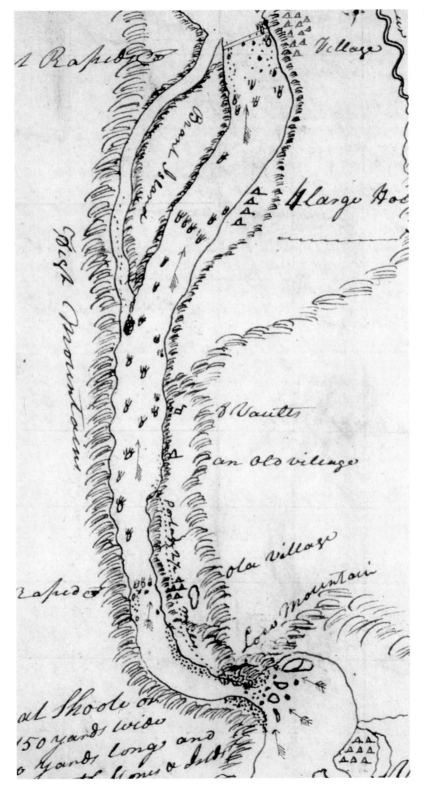

This map by William Clark shows a series of rapids on the Columbia River. When going upstream, the Corps had to portage their canoes around the swift water.

By early May, the Corps was back in Nez Percé land, where they also received a warm welcome. They met their old friend and guide Twisted Hair, and rounded up most of the horses the tribe had kept for them over the winter. They were forced to stay with the Nez Percé for several weeks. Snow was still too deep on the Lolo Trail, which spanned the Bitterroot Mountains.

May 7th 1806. This [is] unwelcom inteligence to men confined to a diet of horsebeef and roots, and who are as anxious as we are to return to the fat plains of the Missouri and thence to our native homes.

MERIWETHER LEWIS

As they waited for the mountain snows to recede, they spent the next four weeks keeping in shape by playing athletic games with the young Nez Percé warriors. They competed in foot races and shooting matches. The Indians were impressed, especially by Captain Lewis's marksmanship. They also played a new game called "base," an early version of baseball.

On horseback, it was the Nez Percé who put the Americans to shame. The Indians rode at breakneck speed, and could shoot arrows at a moving target with pinpoint accuracy, even at a full gallop.

One of the Nez Percé chiefs gave Lewis and Clark horses, and refused to take any payment. At a tribal council, the Nez Percé made a promise that they would always be at peace with Lewis and Clark, and the United States.

On June 10, after four weeks with the Nez Percé, the expedition packed up and set off across Weippe Prairie, heading for the Bitterroots. Chief Twisted Hair told them it was still too snowy up in the mountains, but Lewis and Clark couldn't stand waiting any longer. All the men looked forward to crossing the mountains and descending onto the Great Plains, where herds of buffalo awaited.

June 17, 1806. Here was winter with all it's rigors; the air was cold, my hands and feet were benumbed.

MERIWETHER LEWIS

They soon discovered they had been too hasty. In less than a week they found themselves in snow 12 feet (3.7 m) deep, and couldn't find the trail. For the first time in the entire expedition, they were forced to retreat.

On June 24, they tried again, this time with several Nez Percé, most of them teenage boys. The captains wrote several times of how impressed they were of the woodsman skills of their guides. Food was scarce, the temperatures were freezing, but it was easier going then when they had crossed the year before, thanks in large part to their guides.

By the end of June, they descended to the camp they called Travelers' Rest, at the end of the Lolo Trail. The ordeal of the mountains was finally behind them.

Edward S. Curtis took this picture of a member of the Nez Percé tribe a century after Lewis and Clark passed through tribal lands.

13th July 1806. The indian woman who has been of great Service to me as a pilot through this Country recommends a gap in the mountain more South which I shall cross.

WILLIAM CLARK

DOWN THE YELLOWSTONE

At Travelers' Rest, the captains announced a complicated and daring plan. They would split up the expedition so they could explore more of Louisiana Territory. Lewis knew that President Jefferson would be disappointed that there was no Northwest Passage, no easy water route across the continent. Lewis hoped they could find a better path than the one they took the previous year, when they had traveled westward.

It was a bold scheme, and probably unwise. They would split into small groups and would be hundreds of miles from each other. While Lewis and several volunteers explored a shortcut to the Great Falls of the Missouri, and then searched for the source of the Marias River, most of the men would return to the Three Forks area of the Missouri River. Once at the Three Forks, they would split up again. Some would float down the river to the Great Falls, where they would dig up the boats and supplies they had buried the previous year. Clark would take a small group overland until they hit the Yellowstone River, then rejoin the main expedition where the river emptied into the Missouri.

It was a plan full of danger, but Lewis and Clark now had enough confidence in their men to risk it. They promised to reunite in one month, then said their good-byes.

July 3rd 1806. I took leave of my worthy friend and companion, Capt. Clark and the party that accompanyed him. I could not avoid feeling much concern on this occasion although I hoped this seperation was only momentary.

MERIWETHER LEWIS

Far left: The Yellowstone River winds past a network of sandstone cliffs near present-day Billings, Montana.

159

Artist John Clymer's *A Gangue of Buffalow* shows Clark's group being stopped on the Yellowstone River by a large herd of bison crossing the water.

When Clark's group reached the Three Forks, Sergeant John Ordway and nine men set off downstream in canoes they had buried at the Beaverhead River the previous autumn. All the supplies they had cached were damp but safe.

Clark headed east, traveling overland on horseback. He took with him a small group, including his slave York, Toussaint Charbonneau, Sacagawea, and her baby, Jean Baptiste.

Sacagawea knew the countryside. She had taken trips in the area when she was a young girl. For the first time on the expedition, she acted as an actual guide, showing them a shortcut across today's Bozeman Pass in Montana.

Clark's group reached the Yellowstone River on July 15. They hollowed out two big cottonwood trees to make canoes. In the middle of the night, Indians stole many of their horses.

The group lashed the two canoes together to make a raft, then floated down the Yellowstone. Soon they were on the Great Plains again, with plentiful game to hunt. The men were especially eager to hunt buffalo, which they craved after going so long on a diet of roots, dogs, and horsemeat.

Insect pests were another familiar sight on the Plains. As they floated down one section of the river, Clark wrote that grasshoppers "had destroyed every sprig of grass for miles." Mosquitoes tormented them. "The Mosquetoes," Clark wrote, "are more troublesome than ever we have seen them before."

The animal herds they saw were immense. Once, they had to stop the canoes and wait an hour for a giant herd of buffalo to swim across the river ahead of them.

On July 25, Clark discovered a big sandstone outcropping on the south bank of the river, near present-day Billings, Montana. He called it Pompy's Tower, after Sacagawea's son, Jean Baptiste. Clark had grown fond of the little boy, and nicknamed him "Little Pomp."

Clark climbed up the side of the rock and etched his name and date into the soft sandstone. It is the only physical evidence of the Corps of Discovery that can still be seen today.

Above, top: Pompy's Tower, called Pompeys Pillar today. *Above:* Clark's inscription.

John Clymer's *The Lewis Crossing* shows Lewis and his group crossing the Clark Fork River, near present-day Missoula, Montana. Nez Percé guides helped Lewis part of the way.

THE MARIAS EXPLORATION

As Clark drifted down the Yellowstone River, Lewis was hundreds of miles away to the northwest. After dropping off some of his men at the Great Falls of Montana, his small group set out to explore the Marias River. The terms of the Louisiana Purchase said that the land included the drainage of the Missouri River and all its tributaries. Lewis hoped that the Marias ran far to the north, into Canada. If so, it would give the United States claim to land that England wanted.

Accompanying Lewis were George Drouillard and the two Field brothers, Joseph and Reubin. After several days, they camped near the northernmost reach of the Marias, close to the eastern edge of present-day Glacier National Park.

To Lewis's dismay, the river didn't stretch into Canada. He called the area Camp Disappointment. After two days of rest, he and his small group headed back toward the Missouri River.

They were now deep into Blackfeet Indian country, and Lewis was nervous. Other tribes the Corps had encountered all feared the Blackfeet. They controlled trade on the northern Plains, and they had connections with the British, which meant they were well armed with rifles and horses. Even though Lewis was supposed to set up peaceful trade relations with Native Americans, he hoped to avoid meeting the Blackfeet. He didn't have enough men to defend against an attack if the Blackfeet proved hostile.

On July 26, Lewis looked through his telescope and spied eight Blackfeet warriors watching the Americans. "This was a very unpleasant sight," he later wrote.

Despite his fears, Lewis met with the Indians, giving them gifts of handkerchiefs and peace medals to ease the tension. With nightfall approaching, they all camped under the shade of three small cottonwood trees.

Photographer Edward S. Curtis's *In Blackfoot Country*.

Artist Karl Bodmer painted this Blackfeet portrait in the 1830s.

Lewis told the Indians that the Americans had set up trade with the Shoshones and Nez Percé, and that they also wanted trade relations with the Blackfeet. But the warriors weren't happy. With American trade goods, especially weapons, being handed to their enemies, the Blackfeet monopoly on trade was threatened, their power diminished. Lewis was bringing the worst possible news to the Blackfeet.

At the first light of morning, Lewis was startled awake by shouting. He saw Joseph Field fighting with one of the Blackfeet, who had tried to steal Field's rifle. Reubin Field, while trying to take back his own rifle, had already stabbed one of the Blackfeet to death.

I then drew a pistol from my holster and terning myself about saw the indian making off with my gun. I ran at him with my pistol and bid him lay down my gun, which he was in the act of doing when the Fieldses returned and drew up their guns to shoot him, which I forbade as he did not appear to be about to make any resistance or commit any offensive act, He droped the gun and walked slowly off.

MERIWETHER LEWIS

Lewis recovered his rifle, but two other Blackfeet were rounding up the men's horses. Lewis ran to stop them. One hid behind a rock. As Lewis ran forward, the other warrior wheeled about, rifle in hand.

At the distance of 30 steps . . . I shot him through the belly, he fell to his knees and on his wright elbow from which position he partly raised himself up and fired at me, and turning himself about crawled in behind a rock. . . . He overshot me, [but] being bearheaded I felt the wind of his bullet very distinctly.

MERIWETHER LEWIS

Lewis and his men got their weapons back, but two Blackfeet were dead. The other six warriors had fled, running off toward their main camp. Lewis was sure a war party would soon be chasing them, looking for revenge. He and his men immediately rounded up their horses and set off in a rush across the prairie.

They ran their horses for 24 hours, continuing even in the dark of night. After fleeing for 120 miles (193 km), they finally made it to the Missouri River.

As if by a miracle, at that moment they met the combined expedition groups from the Great Falls, rounding a bend in the river. Lewis and his men abandoned their horses and leaped into the canoes. Then they were off, racing downriver to safety.

Frontier artist Karl Bodmer painted this portrait of a Piegan warrior. The Piegans were members of the Blackfeet tribe.

*17ᵗʰ September 1806. This Gentleman
informed us that we had been long Since
given [up] by the people of the US . . . and
almost forgotton. [But] the President of the
U. States had yet hopes of us.*

WILLIAM CLARK

JOURNEY'S END

On August 12, the two groups of explorers linked up near the confluence of the Missouri and Yellowstone Rivers. The two captains traded stories of their adventures and narrow escapes. The only major injury had happened to Lewis a few days earlier. While out hunting, one-eyed Pierre Cruzatte mistook Lewis for an elk and shot him in the buttocks. The bullet entered one cheek and passed through the other. It was a painful wound, but Lewis was walking again in three weeks. During his recovery he had to lie on his belly in a canoe.

The Corps sailed down the swift-flowing current of the Missouri, sometimes covering more than 80 miles (129 km) a day. Two days after meeting at the Yellowstone, they stopped at the Mandan villages to visit their old friends. They gave Charbonneau his pay, and said good-bye to Sacagawea and her son. Clark had grown fond of Jean Baptiste, a "butifull promising child." He offered to raise and educate him back East. Clark later wrote, "They observed that in one year the boy would be Sufficiently old to leave his mother . . . if I would be so friendly as to raise the Child . . . in such a manner as I thought proper, to which I agreed."

The men of the Corps also said good-bye to one of their own, John Colter. He had fallen in love with the wild frontier, and wanted to join two trappers who were planning to go up the Yellowstone to hunt for beaver. The captains granted Colter an early discharge. He later became one of the first mountain men, and the first white man to see what is today Yellowstone National Park.

An 1870 photo of Yellowstone National Park's Old Faithful geyser, by William Henry Jackson.

Olaf Carl Seltzer's
*Prowlers of the
Prairie.*

After a three-day stay with the Mandans, the Corps
proceeded on once more. They practically flew down the river,
eager to be home. As they passed the lands of the Teton Sioux,
the tribe that had given them so much trouble in the autumn
of 1804, they saw Chief Black Buffalo hailing them from a
hilltop. The Corps refused to stop. Clark shouted to the chief,
telling him they remembered how poorly they had been
treated, and that the Teton Sioux were "bad people." In
response, Black Buffalo cursed the Corps by striking his rifle
three times on the ground.

Near present-day Sioux City, Iowa, they stopped to pay
their respects to Sergeant Charles Floyd. He was the only
expedition member to die during the trip, a miracle
considering all the hardships they had endured.

As they sped home with the current, they began encountering boats coming upriver, traders and fur trappers hoping to profit in the new territories. The Lewis and Clark expedition had opened a floodgate of exploration and settlement. The men eagerly listened to news of the past two and a half years. They also learned that most people back home had given them up for dead.

On September 20, the men saw a cow grazing near shore. They raised a cheer: it was the first sign that they were approaching civilization. When they reached the tiny outpost of La Charette, the citizens were "much astonished in seeing us return."

On September 23, 1806, the men of the Corps of Discovery spent their last day together. They arrived at the mouth of the Missouri River, then drifted downstream on the Mississippi, stopping briefly at Camp Dubois, where they had spent the winter of 1803-1804.

Karl Bodmer painted this scene of Missouri River traders and their keelboat. As Lewis and Clark came down the Missouri in 1806, they met many boats filled with traders and fur trappers heading into Louisiana Territory.

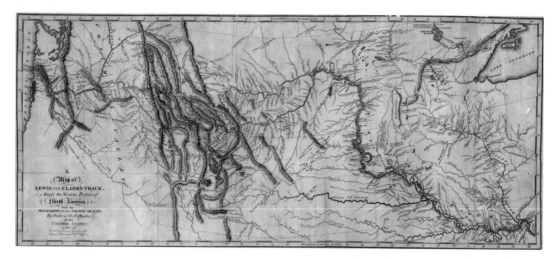

This is William Clark's map of North America, which many consider a masterpiece of cartography. To draw the map, he combined compass readings, distances, and sketches he drew while on the journey. He also used information from Indians, traders, and other explorers.

At noon they came within sight of St. Louis. After 8,000 miles (12,875 km) and 28 months, Lewis and Clark had returned! The entire town gathered on shore to watch and celebrate.

Fired three rounds as we approached . . . and landed oppocit the center of the Town. The people gathred on the Shore and Huzzared three cheers . . . then the party considerable much rejoiced that we have the Expedition Completed.

And now we look for boarding in Town and wait for our settlement, and then we entend to return to our native homes to See our parents once more, as we have been So long from them.
JOHN ORDWAY

The country treated them like national heroes. It was as if they had returned from the moon. Lewis made his report to a grateful President Jefferson. As a reward, Congress awarded the men double pay, plus 320 acres (129 hectares) of land. The captains each received 1,600 acres (647 hectares).

Lewis and Clark and the Corps of Discovery were trailblazers, the first United States citizens to cross the continent. They were the first to explore uncharted territory west of the Mississippi. They mapped the land, described 178 plants and 122 animals new to science, and met with dozens of Native American tribes. It was their great journey that opened the West to American expansion. This band of heroes uncovered a land rich with possibilities. Two hundred years later, we still follow in their footsteps.

The work we are now doing is, I trust, done for posterity, in such a way that they need not repeat it. . . . We shall delineate with correctness the great arteries of this great country; those who come after us will . . . fill up the canvas we begin.

THOMAS JEFFERSON

THEY PROCEEDED ON

MERIWETHER LEWIS (1774-1809)

After co-commanding the Corps of Discovery, Lewis became governor of Louisiana Territory while living in St. Louis. It wasn't a job he was suited for. He was also unlucky in love. He courted several women, but was turned down each time. Lewis drank heavily. He also suffered from depression, made worse by an addiction to opium, which he took to fight malaria.

President Jefferson had urged Lewis to prepare his journals of the expedition for publication. Lewis made arrangements with a publisher in Philadelphia, and had several drawings made of new animals and plants discovered on the expedition. But he never finished preparing the journals. Historian Stephen Ambrose said that Lewis "developed the writer's block of all time." Nobody knows why Lewis had such difficulties finishing the journals. As time went on, Lewis became more and more depressed. He lost money in land deals and became involved in a questionable fur-trade business. He had to borrow money, and creditors began hounding him.

In 1809 Lewis traveled to Washington, D.C., to straighten out his financial problems. Along the way, he became more and more distraught over his troubles. On a trail called the Natchez Trace in Tennessee, Meriwether Lewis, at the age of 35, took his own life.

WILLIAM CLARK (1770-1838)

Clark served as the governor of Missouri Territory from 1813-1821. He lived in St. Louis with his wife, Julia, the same woman he had named a river after during the expedition. Together they had five children. After Julia's death, Clark remarried, this time to a widow. Clark adopted her three children, and together they had two more, for a total of ten children.

From 1813 until his death, Clark was in charge of Indian affairs west of the Mississippi River. Native Americans, most of whom considered him their good friend, called Clark "the Red-Headed Chief." Many came to visit him in St. Louis. Clark once wrote to President Jefferson to say he was sorry he couldn't do more to help the plight of the Native Americans.

After an eight-day illness in 1838, William Clark died at the age of 69 in the home of his eldest son, Meriwether Lewis Clark.

SACAGAWEA (c.1788-1812?)

Not much is known about Sacagawea's life after the expedition. She continued living with her husband, Toussaint Charbonneau, at the Knife River Indian villages. In 1809 they traveled to St. Louis with their son, Jean Baptiste. William Clark became the boy's guardian. In 1812, at Fort Manuel in present-day South Dakota, she gave birth to a baby girl, Lisette. That winter, still in her early 20's, Sacagawea became ill and died. (There are legends that Sacagawea died in 1884, near the age of 100, on the Wind River Shoshone Reservation in Wyoming. Most historians, however, believe she died at Fort Manuel. And in the 1820's, William Clark made a list of the status of all the expedition members. He reported that Sacagawea had already died by that time.)

TOUSSAINT CHARBONNEAU (c.1758-?)

After the expedition, Sacagawea's husband did work for Manuel Lisa's Missouri River Fur Company. He also worked as an interpreter for explorers, artists, and the U.S. government. He lived most of his life with the Mandan and Hidatsa Indians. Charbonneau died sometime around the age of 80.

JEAN BAPTISTE CHARBONNEAU (1805-1866)

Sacagawea and Toussaint Charbonneau's son was sent to live in St. Louis at the age of 6. William Clark had offered to raise the boy and provide him with a good education. By the time he was 20 he could speak Hidatsa, Shoshone, French, English, Greek, and Latin. In 1824 he met Prince Paul of Wurttemberg, who taught him to speak German, and took him on a six-year tour of Europe, where he dined with royalty, learned to speak Italian, and once played violin with Beethoven. After returning home, Jean Baptiste became a fur trapper and mountain man. He also served as a guide and interpreter to other explorers and soldiers. He moved to California, but later decided to seek his fortune in the gold fields of Montana. He died of pneumonia on his way through Oregon in 1866, at the age of 61.

YORK (c.1770-1832?)

In 1811, several years after the expedition, William Clark finally granted York his freedom. York started a freighting business in Tennessee and Kentucky. He probably died of cholera sometime around 1832.

GEORGE DROUILLARD (?-1810)

George Drouillard, the expedition's best hunter, joined the Missouri River Fur Company. In 1810 he helped establish Manuel Lisa's trading post at Three Forks. While there, Drouillard was killed in a fight with Blackfeet Indians.

IF YOU GO TODAY

MONTICELLO

Thomas Jefferson's domed house at Monticello is one of the most distinctive buildings in America. Jefferson was an amateur architect who planned and supervised every detail in the construction of his mountaintop home.

Situated in Albemarle County, near Charlottesville, Virginia, Monticello is part of a 5,000-acre (2,023-ha) plantation that Jefferson inherited when he was 14 years old. The grounds surrounding his home were devoted to Jefferson's personal garden, a living laboratory where he studied plants from around the world. Today the vegetable garden shares space with flower gardens, a fruit garden, orchards, vineyards, and a multitude of trees, Jefferson's favorite garden plants.

Jefferson was constantly upgrading and remodeling Monticello. He began construction in 1768. He completely remodeled it starting in 1796, and finished by the time he retired from public life in 1809. Today Monticello is recognized as an international treasure, the only house in America on the United Nations' World Heritage List of sites to be protected at all costs.

Guided tours inside Monticello are entertaining and revealing. The entrance hall contains many American Indian artifacts and natural history specimens, including several from the Lewis & Clark expedition.

Monticello is open every day of the year, including Sundays, except Christmas. It is located two miles (3.2 km) southeast of Charlottesville, approximately 125 miles (201 km) from Washington, D.C., and 110 miles (177 km) from Williamsburg, Virginia. Tickets entitle visitors to a 30-minute guided tour of the home, access to the Museum Shop, and self-directed tours of the grounds. Guided tours of the gardens and grounds are also available.

For more information, visit Monticello's web site at: *http://www.monticello.org*, or call *804-977-1783*. For information specific to the Lewis & Clark expedition, go to: *http://www.monticello.org/jefferson/lewisandclark/index.html*

AMERICAN PHILOSOPHICAL SOCIETY

The American Philosophical Society is the nation's oldest scholarly society, founded in Philadelphia, Pennsylvania, by Benjamin Franklin in 1743. Thomas Jefferson sent Meriwether Lewis here to learn from the nation's top scientists before embarking on the Corps of Discovery. Most of the Lewis and Clark journals, along with other artifacts from the expedition, are housed at the Society's headquarters building, located in Independence National Historical Park, around the corner from Independence Hall and the Liberty Bell.

Exhibitions in Philosophical Hall are open to the public. Information on current exhibits can be found at: *http://www.amphilsoc.org/exhibitions*. For a comprehensive list of illustrations that appear in the journals of Lewis and Clark, go to: *http://www.amphilsoc.org/library/guides/lcills.htm*

LEWIS & CLARK INTERPRETIVE CENTER, WOOD RIVER/HARTFORD, ILLINOIS

The main exhibition hall of the Lewis & Clark Interpretive Center in Wood River/Hartford, Illinois, contains 14,000 square feet of interior exhibits, a replica of

Camp River Dubois, and a multi-media theater. It also features a full-scale 55-foot (16.8 m) cutaway replica of the Corps of Discovery's keelboat (left). *New Poag Road, Illinois Route 3, Hartford, IL 62048; 618-251-5811; or contact the Greater Alton/Twin Rivers Convention & Visitors Bureau; 1-800-258-6645; http://www.visitalton.org*

St. Louis, Missouri

The city of St. Louis hosts several sites pertaining to Lewis and Clark. Beneath the 630-foot (192 m) stainless steel Gateway Arch (left) is the **Museum of Westward Expansion**, which includes exhibits and photographs related to the Corps of Discovery. *Jefferson National Expansion Memorial, 11 North 4th Street, St. Louis, MO 63102; 314-425-4465; http://www.nps.gov/jeff/mus-tour.htm*

The **Missouri Historical Society** has four floors of exhibits and artifacts featuring Lewis and Clark, Indian culture, and the westward migration of early pioneers. *Jefferson Memorial Building, Forest Park, St. Louis, MO 63108; 314-746-4599; http://www.mohistory.org*

Bellefontaine Cemetery is the final resting place of William Clark (right), plus other historical figures. The cemetery is located about five miles north of downtown St. Louis. Maps are available at the cemetery office. *4947 W. Florissant Ave., St. Louis, MO; 314-381-0750*

Lewis & Clark Center, St. Charles, Missouri

This museum, in historic St. Charles, MO, includes dioramas and exhibits explaining the expedition. *701 Riverside Drive, St. Charles, MO 63301; 636-947-3199*

National Frontier Trails Center, Independence, Missouri

The Lewis and Clark trail is one of four major routes highlighted at this museum, which presents the story of exploration and settlement of the American West. Also included are the Oregon, Santa Fe, and California trails. *318 West Pacific, Independence, MO 64050; 816-325-7575; http://www.frontiertrailscenter.com*

Lewis and Clark State Park, Onawa, Iowa

On a small oxbow lake about five miles (8 km) west of the town of Onawa, Iowa, is a full-scale copy of the expedition's keelboat (right). There are also reproductions of the two pirogues that travelled along up the Missouri River. *712-423-2829*

Lewis & Clark: Adventures West

Sergeant Floyd Monument

Sergeant Floyd, the only fatality of the Corps of Discovery, is buried on a bluff overlooking the Missouri River near Sioux City, Iowa. The grave is marked with a 100-foot (30.5 m) obelisk (left). Informative plaques tell the story of the expedition. *I-29, exit 143; 801 Fourth Street, Sioux City, IA 51102*

Also in Sioux City, at the **Sergeant Floyd Riverboat Museum and Welcome Center**, are 19th century photographs of Floyd's grave, copies of Clark's maps, and other items from the expedition. *I-29, exit 149 to 1000 S. Larsen Park Rd., Sioux City, IA 51104-4914; 712-279-0198*

Fort Mandan

The Lewis and Clark Interpretive Center, in Washburn, North Dakota (just north of Bismarck) is loaded with artifacts and artwork covering the Corps of Discovery, including a complete 81-print collection of famed frontier artist Karl Bodmer. Nearby is a reconstruction of Fort Mandan, where the expedition spent the winter of 1804-05. Included are living history demonstrations.

PO Box 607, Washburn, ND 58577-0607; 701-462-8535; http://www.fortmandan.org

Knife River Indian Villages National Historic Site

One-half mile (.8 km) north of Stanton, North Dakota, is the **Knife River Indian Villages National Historic Site**, which preserves the remains of three Hidatsa Native American settlements. More than 50 archaeological sites lead scientists and historians to believe that the Knife River settlements may have been occupied for as long as 8,000 years, ending with 500 years of Hidatsa earthlodge village occupation. The 1,758-acre (711-hectare) site preserves the culture and agricultural lifestyle of the North American Plains Indians. Circular depressions on the ground mark where earthlodges once stood, some as big as 40 feet (12 m) in diameter. Cultural and historical exhibits at the site include an earth lodge reproduction (left). *PO Box 9, Stanton, ND 58571; 701-745-3300; http://www.nps.gov/knri*

WILD & SCENIC MISSOURI RIVER

Canoe Montana, in Fort Benton, Montana, arranges expeditions along one of the last unspoiled sections of the Missouri River. A three- or five-day White Cliffs tour includes great scenery and wildlife viewing. Experienced guides help out along the way. Single-day tours are also available. *1312 Front Street, P.O. Box 591, Fort Benton, MT 59442; 1-800-500-4538; http://www.montanariver.com*

LEWIS & CLARK NATIONAL HISTORIC TRAIL INTERPRETIVE CENTER

Located in Great Falls, Montana, on a bluff overlooking the Missouri River, this is one of the best museums along the Lewis & Clark trail. While the Corps of Discovery's portage around the Great Falls is featured (left), many other aspects of the expedition are covered, including Native American culture. The exhibits are self-guided, but costumed living-history interpreters answer any questions you might have, and they perform interesting demonstrations. *4201 Giant Springs Road, Great Falls, MT 59403;406-727-8733; http://www.fs.fed.us/r1/lewisclark/lcic.htm*

LEMHI PASS NATIONAL HISTORIC LANDMARK

Lemhi Pass National Historic Landmark (right) straddles the Continental Divide on the Montana-Idaho border. It is the site where Meriwether Lewis discovered there was no easy water route from coast to coast. Instead, when he reached the top of the ridgeline, he later wrote, "I discovered

immence ranges of high mountains still to the West of us with their tops partially covered with snow." Lemhi Pass today is much as it was when the Corps of Discovery passed by in 1805. It is about 12 miles (19 km) east of the town of Tendoy, Idaho, on a dusty, bumpy road that can be difficult to drive on, especially after a rainstorm. The U.S. Forest Service maintains signposts that tell the story of the pass. *406-683-3900; http://www.fs.fed.us/r1/b-d/virtualtours/lemhi-pass/virtual-lemhi-pass.html*

BEAVERHEAD ROCK STATE PARK, MT

Beaverhead Rock (left) is the landmark that Sacagawea recognized from her childhood as the Corps struggled up the Jefferson River. It is still visible today. Beaverhead Rock State Park is located about 13 miles (21 km) north of the town of Dillon, Montana, on MT Highway 41. *406-944-4042*

LOLO TRAIL

Together with Lemhi Pass and a small section of the Missouri River east of Fort Benton, Montana, the Lolo Trail is very close to how Lewis & Clark saw the West in 1805. Access is off U.S. Highway 12 west of Lolo, Montana. A small section of the actual trail (right) can be hiked near Highway 12, but most of the Lolo follows a ridgeline north of the road. The trail itself can be followed closely along the Lolo Motorway, which follows Forest Service Road 500. It's very rough, and you'll need a high-clearance vehicle, preferably one with 4-wheel drive. Original campsites and historic points are marked. The trail is open during the summer months, July through September. Check with the Forest Service for weather and road conditions, *209-476-4541*. You can also explore the trail by horseback: *Triple "O" Outfitters, 208-464-2349 or 208-464-2761; http://www.tripleo-outfitters.com/trips/lolo*

FORT CLATSOP NATIONAL MEMORIAL

Built in 1955, the reconstruction of Fort Clatsop (left) sits near the original site of the Corps of Discovery's 1805-1806 winter quarters. Run today by the National Park Service, Fort Clatsop is based on a floor plan drawn by William Clark on the elkhide cover of his fieldbook. Living history demonstrations show many of the frontier skills used by the Corps. In addition to touring the fort, you can also hike on trails leading to the expedition's canoe landing and the spring where they drew their fresh water. The fort is located 4.5 miles (7 km) southwest of Astoria, Oregon. *503-861-2471; http://www.nps.gov/focl*

ECOLA STATE PARK, CANNON BEACH, OR

Cannon Beach is where the Corps found the remains of a whale that had washed up on shore. Today this is a day-use park where you can see bird rookeries, sea lions, and herds of elk. There is also a scenic cliff hiking trail over Tillamook Head. *503-368-5154*

COLUMBIA RIVER GORGE NATIONAL SCENIC AREA

The Columbia River Gorge is a river canyon that cuts a water route through the Cascade Mountain Range. There are over 50 miles (80 km) of attractions on both the Washington and Oregon sides of the gorge, including spectacular waterfalls, state parks, campsites, wildflower viewing, hiking trails, water sports, and many other outdoor activities. At Bonneville Dam, you can take a tour of the dam that inundated the cascades of the Columbia River. There is also a fish hatchery, trails, and a Lewis & Clark exhibit. *541-374-8820*

Multnomah Falls (above), is one of many world-famous waterfalls along the Columbia River Scenic Highway, a winding, scenic 22-mile (35 km) road that runs parallel to I-84. *http://www.odot.state.or.us/hcrh*

The Columbia Gorge Discovery Center at The Dalles, Oregon, contains exhibits on local history as well as Lewis & Clark, and also features trails and picnic areas. *541-296-8600; http://www.gorgediscovery.org*

POMPEYS PILLAR NATIONAL MONUMENT

William Clark carved his name partway up this 150-foot (46 m) sandstone outcropping (right) on July 25, 1806. Named after Sacagawea's son, the pillar overlooks the Yellowstone River. It is situated about 25 miles (40 km) east of Billings, Montana, just off Interstate 94. The site includes a small visitor center, picnic grounds, and a stairway leading to Clark's signature and continuing to the top. *406-875-2233; http://www.mt.blm.gov/pillarmon/general.html*

* For detailed directions to these and other sites along the Lewis & Clark Trail, the author heartily recommends *Along the Trail With Lewis and Clark*, by Barbara Fifer and Vicky Soderberg. The book also includes historical highlights and maps.

Lewis & Clark: Adventures West

A January sunrise over the Missouri River, near the reconstructed Fort Mandan site in Washburn, North Dakota, part of the Lewis & Clark Interpretive Center.

GLOSSARY

CACHE

A place where explorers hide food and supplies. Lewis and Clark cached supplies and canoes in several places, including the Beaverhead River and at the Great Falls of Montana. Knowing that they would return along the same route, they buried items they couldn't use the rest of the way westward, such as the large oversized canoes called pirgoues. They also cached many of the scientific specimens they collected. On at least one occasion river water seeped into a cache, ruining many of the specimens and notes.

CHRONOMETER

A scientific instrument used to measure time precisely. By knowing the exact time and measuring the position of the sun, Lewis & Clark were able to make accurate readings of the expedition's longitude, the distance east or west on the earth's surface.

CONTINENTAL DIVIDE

A ridge of the Rocky Mountains in North America. Water flowing east of the divide eventually finds its way to the Atlantic Ocean. Water flowing west goes to the Pacific Ocean.

CORPS

A branch of the military that has a specialized function.

DEAD RECKONING

A way of estimating distance based on data in a written logbook, such as speed and time spent going in a certain direction. For example, when travelling upriver, one might estimate that a certain bend in the river is a mile away. Once you get to the bend, you estimate the distance to the next bend, or other landmark, like a big tree or island. At the end of the day, you add up all the figures to get the total distance travelled on the river. Some people are very skilled at dead reckoning. William Clark estimated that near the mouth of the Columbia River the Corps had travelled 4,142 miles (6,666 km) from St. Louis. Scientists using more precise methods later showed that Clark was only 40 miles (64 km) off!

Lewis & Clark: Adventures West

DEPRESSION

An emotional condition, often caused by a chemical imbalance in the brain, that causes feelings of hopelessness and sadness. Meriwether Lewis likely suffered from bouts of depression.

FEDERALIST PARTY

A political party in the U.S., from 1789-1816, that favored a strong, centralized government. Alexander Hamilton and President John Adams were prominent Federalists.

FLINTLOCK

An old-fashioned rifle or pistol in which a flint in the hammer strikes a piece of metal, which produces a spark that ignites the gunpowder.

GREAT PLAINS

A huge, sloping region of valleys and plains in west-central North America. The Great Plains extend from Texas to southern Canada, and from the Rocky Mountains nearly 400 miles (644 km) to the east.

HEADWATERS

The beginning of a large stream or river.

KEELBOAT

A large, shallow-hulled freight boat used extensively in the 18th and 19th centuries on the Mississippi and Missouri Rivers.

NORTHWEST PASSAGE

The fabled easy water route across North America from the Atlantic to the Pacific Ocean.

PASS

A path used to cross a mountain ridge that divides two watersheds. For example, the Lemhi Pass crosses the Continental Divide—water running down the east side finds its way to the Atlantic Ocean, while water on the west side flows to the Pacific Ocean. Passes are usually low points between two higher peaks. "Divide" and "saddle" are other words for pass.

PIROGUE

A large boat used to carry cargo, powered by oars, or sometimes a sail. The Corps of Discovery used two pirogues to supplement the larger keelboat on the journey up the Missouri River in 1804. In 1805, the pirogues continued upriver as far as Great Falls, Montana.

PLAINS INDIANS

Native Americans who lived on the Great Plains of North America. They spoke different languages, but shared many cultural traits, such as a nomadic following of bison herds. Tribes include the Sioux, Cheyenne, Blackfeet, and many others.

PORTAGE

To carry a boat and supplies overland from one lake or river to another. It can be a difficult and grueling process, depending on the terrain. The Corps of Discovery portaged around the Great Falls of Montana for over 18 miles (29 km).

REPUBLICAN PARTY

A former U.S. political party organized by Thomas Jefferson in 1792. (Today's Republican Party was formed in 1854 to oppose the extension of slavery.)

VERMILION

A bright red powder, made of mercuric sulfide, that is used as a pigment. Native Americans used it to make face paint, trading with white settlers for the prized powder. Native Americans had their own methods of making red pigment, but vermilion powder was easiest to obtain and use.

The front gate of the reconstructed Fort Mandan, near Washburn, North Dakota.

Lewis & Clark: Adventures West

FURTHER READING

Ambrose, Stephen E. *Lewis & Clark: Voyage of Discovery*. National Geographic Society, 1998.

Ambrose, Stephen E. *Undaunted Courage: Meriwether Lewis, Thomas Jefferson, and the Opening of the American West.* Simon & Schuster, 1996.

Appelman, Roy. *Lewis and Clark: Historic Places Associated with Their Transcontinental Exploration.* National Park Service, 1975.

Bakeless, John. *Lewis & Clark: Partners in Discovery.* Dover Publications, 1996.

Bartlett, Richard A., and Goetzmann, William H. *Exploring the American West: 1803–1879: Handbook 116.* National Park Service, 1982.

Betts, Robert B. *In Search of York: The Slave Who Went to the Pacific with Lewis and Clark.* Colorado Associated University Press, 1985.

Carrick, Michael F. "Meriwether Lewis's Air Gun." *We Proceeded On*, vol. 28, no. 4 (November 2002).

Chuinard, Eldon G. *Only One Man Died: Medical Aspects of the Lewis and Clark Expedition.* Arthur Clark Co., 1980.

DeVoto, Bernard. *The Course of Empire.* Houghton Mifflin, 1952.

DeVoto, Bernard, ed. *The Journals of Lewis and Clark.* Houghton Mifflin, 1953.

Duncan, Dayton, et al. *Lewis & Clark: The Journey of the Corps of Discovery: An Illustrated History.* Alfred A. Knopf, 1997.

Duncan, Dayton. *Out West: An American Journey.* Viking Penguin, 1987.

Fanselow, Julie. *Traveling the Lewis & Clark Trail.* Falcon Publishing, 1994.

Fifer, Barara, and Soderberg, Vicky. *Along the Trail with Lewis and Clark.* Montana Magazine, 1998.

Fifer, Barbara. *Going Along With Lewis & Clark.* Montana Magazine, 2000.

Gass, Patrick. *A Journal of the Voyages and Travels of a Corps of Discovery Under the Command of Capt. Lewis and Capt. Clark.* Ross & Haines, 1958.

Gibbons, Loren M. "All Them Horses and One Poor Mule." *We Proceeded On*, vol. 28, no. 3 (August 2002).

Holmberg, James J., ed. *Dear Brother: Letters of William Clark to Jonathan Clark.* Yale University Press, 2002.

Jenkinson, Clay S. *The Character of Meriwether Lewis.* Marmarth Press, 2000.

Jenkinson, Clay S. *A Lewis and Clark Chapbook: Lewis and Clark in North Dakota.* North Dakota Humanities Council, 2002

Moulton, Gary E., ed. *The Journals of the Lewis and Clark Expedition.* University of Nebraska Press, 1988.

Ronda, James P. *Lewis and Clark Among the Indians.* University of Nebraska Press, 1984.

Saindon, Robert A. "The 'Unhappy Affair' on Two Medicine River." *We Proceeded On*, vol. 28, no. 3 (August 2002).

Schmidt, Thomas. *National Geographic's Guide to the Lewis & Clark Trail.* National Geographic Society, 1998.

Schmidt, Thomas, and Schmidt, Jeremy. *The Saga of Lewis & Clark: Into the Uncharted West.* DK Publishing, 1999.

Thorp, Daniel B. *Lewis & Clark: An American Journey.* Michael Friedman Publishing Group, Inc. 1998.

Walcheck, Kenneth C. "Tales of the Veriegated Bear." *We Proceeded On*, vol. 28, no. 4 (November 2002).

PICTURE CREDITS

p 1 bronze sculpture by Bob Scriver, Great Falls, Montana, John Hamilton

p 9 mule deer, North Dakota, John Hamilton

p 10 *Lewis and Clark, 1804*, L. Edward Fisher, Missouri Bankers Association

p 11 prairie grass, North Dakota, John Hamilton

p 12 herd of bison grazing, North Dakota, John Hamilton

p 13 *Lewis's First View of the Rockies*, Olaf Seltzer, Gilcrease Museum

p 14 cliffs at Fort Benton, Montana, John Hamilton

p 15 *Thomas Jefferson*, courtesy Independence National Historical Park

p 18 waterfall, Columbia River Gorge, Oregon, John Hamilton

p 19 *Meriwether Lewis*, C.W. Peale, courtesy Independence National Historical Park

p 20 *Captain Meriwether Lewis*, Charles B.J.F. Saint-Mémin, courtesy New York Historical Society

p 21 Monticello, Virginia John Hamilton

p 22 wildflowers, Pacific shoreline, Oregon, John Hamilton

p 23 *A Topographic Sketch of the Missouri and Upper Mississippi*, Antoine Soulard, Beinecke Rare Book and Manuscript Library, Yale University

p 24 *Oasis in the Bad Lands*, Edward S. Curtis, Library of Congress

p 25 code matrix, Library of Congress

p 26 upper left: provisions, National Archives; lower right: compass, John Hamilton

p 27 Model 1803 rifle, Buffalo Bill Historical Center, Cody, Wyoming

p 28 Missouri River, Niobrara State Park, Nebraska, John Hamilton

p 29 *William Clark*, C.W. Peale, courtesy Independence National Historical Park

p 30 gray wolf, Grizzly and Wolf Discovery Center, West Yellowstone, Montana, John Hamilton

p 31 *Great Falls of the Columbia River*, William Clark, American Philosophical Society

p 32 sculpture by Bob Scriver, Fort Benton, Montana, John Hamilton

p 33 rainbow, plains of Montana after thunderstorm, John Hamilton

p 37 *A Herd of Bison Crossing the Missouri River*, William Jacob Hays, Sr., Buffalo Bill Historical Center, Cody, Wyoming

p 38 Missouri River, near Boonville, Missouri, John Hamilton

p 39 meat roasting over fire, John Hamilton

p 40 keelboat, William Clark, Beinecke Rare Book and Manuscript Library, Yale University

p 41 Camp Dubois, Lewis and Clark State Historic Site and Park, Hartford, Illinois, John Hamilton

p 42 sandbars, Missouri River, Ponca State Park, Nebraska, John Hamilton

p 43 Charles A. Morganthaler, St. Charles County Historical Society

p 44 iron-framed canoe, John Hamilton

p 45 reenactor playing George Drouillard, John Hamilton

p 46 wildflowers, Missouri River, Niobrara State Park, Nebraska, John Hamilton

p 47 Jim Ollhoff on keelboat, Lewis & Clark State Park, Onawa, Iowa, John Hamilton

p 48 white salmon trout, Codex J: 133, vol. 6, p. 422, neg. 940, American Philosophical Society.

p 50 *Mano Tope (Four Bears)*, George Catlin

p 51 *Painted lodges—Piegan*, Edward S. Curtis, Library of Congress

p 52 upper left: Jefferson peace medal, John Hamilton (both); bottom, left to right:

The Old Cheyenne, Piegan Dandy, Ready for the "Okipe" Buffalo Dance—Mandan, Edward S. Curtis (all), Library of Congress

p 53 *Buffalo Hunt Chase*, George Catlin

p 54 Great Plains, North Dakota, John Hamilton

p 55 pronghorn, South Dakota, John Hamilton

p 56 prairie dogs, North Dakota, John Hamilton

p 57 snake, North Dakota, John Hamilton

p 58 earth lodge, Knife River Indian Villages National Historic Site, North Dakota, John Hamilton

p 59 confluence of Missouri and Bad Rivers, Pierre, South Dakota, John Hamilton

p 60 *Hollow Horn Bear*, Edward S. Curtis, Library of Congress

p 61 *Sioux Council*, George Catlin

p 62 earth lodge interior, Knife River Indian Villages National Historic Site, North Dakota, John Hamilton

p 63 upper right: *Mato-Tope (Four Bears)*, Karl Bodmer; lower right: frozen Missouri River, North Dakota, John Hamilton

p 64 reenactor Mike Scholl, Fort Mandan, North Dakota, John Hamilton

p 65 upper right: *Black Moccasin*, George Catlin; bottom: *Mih-Tutta-Hang-Kusch, Mandan Village*, Karl Bodmer, courtesy Joslyn Art Museum, Omaha, Nebraska

p 66 *Big Medicine*, Charles M. Russell, Montana Historical Society

p 67 upper right: battle ax, Meriwether Lewis, American Philosophical Society; bottom: *The Bison Dance of the Mandan Indians*, Karl Bodmer

p 68 *Sacajawea*, Edward S. Paxson, courtesy State University of Montana Library

p 69 *Nez Perce Babe*, Edward S.

Curtis, Library of Congress

p 71 rainbow over plains of Montana, John Hamilton

pp 72-73 Cliffs at Fort Benton, Montana, John Hamilton

p 74 pelicans at confluence of Yellowstone and Missouri Rivers, North Dakota, John Hamilton

p 75 grizzly bear, Grizzly and Wolf Discovery Center, West Yellowstone, Montana, John Hamilton

p 76 top: *Hasty Retreat*, John Clymer, courtesy Mrs. Doris S. Clymer, and The Clymer Museum of Art; bottom left: reenactor with rifle, John Hamilton

p 77 Missouri River rapids, Great Falls, Montana, John Hamilton

p 78 confluence of Missouri and Marias Rivers, near Loma, Montana, John Hamilton

p 79 *View of the Stone Walls on the Upper Missouri*, Karl Bodmer, courtesy Joslyn Art Museum, Omaha, Nebraska

p 80 map of Marias and Missouri Rivers, William Clark, Beinecke Rare Book and Manuscript Library, Yale University

p 81 reenactor playing Drouillard, John Hamilton

p 82 Rainbow Falls, Great Falls, Montana, John Hamilton

p 83 *The Great Falls of the Missouri*, F.J. Haynes, Montana Historical Society

p 84 prickly pear cactus, John Hamilton

p 85 Draught of the falls and portage of the Missouri River, William Clark, American Philosophical Society

p 86 Three Forks of the Missouri River, John Hamilton

p 87 William Clark field notes, June 2 to July 10, 1805, Beinecke Rare Book and Manuscript Library, Yale University

p 88 Gates of the Rocky Mountains, Montana, John Hamilton

187

INDEX

189

An Appaloosa horse grazes near a replica of Fort Mandan, the expedition's wintering quarters of 1804-1805, near present-day Washburn, North Dakota.